ADOBE PHOTOSHOP CC 2018

STEP BY STEP TRAINING

Learn by doing step by step exercises.
Includes downloadable class files that work on Mac & PC.

D1531699

EDITION 1

Published by:

Noble Desktop LLC
594 Broadway, Suite 1202
New York, NY 10012
www.nobledesktop.com

Table of Contents

Table of Contents

SECTION 3

Table of Contents

Table of Contents

Table of Contents

Downloading the Class Files

Thank You for Purchasing a Noble Desktop Course Workbook!

These instructions tell you how to install the class files you'll need to go through the exercises in this workbook.

Downloading & Installing Class Files

1. Navigate to the **Desktop**.

2. Create a **new folder** called **Class Files** (this is where you'll put the files after they have been downloaded).

3. Go to nobledesktop.com/download

4. Enter the code **ps-1712-07**

5. If you haven't already, click **Start Download**.

6. After the **.zip** file has finished downloading, be sure to unzip the file if it hasn't been done for you. You should end up with a **Photoshop Class** folder.

7. Drag the downloaded folder into the **Class Files** folder you just made. These are the files you will use while going through the workbook.

8. If you still have the downloaded .zip file, you can delete that. That's it! Enjoy.

The Tools Panel Expanded & Keyboard Shortcuts

We included several PDFs in **Desktop > Class Files > Photoshop Class** that you can refer to in this class as well as your future Photoshop adventures.

The Tools Panel Expanded (Find Hidden Tools)

To save space in the **Tools** panel, Adobe hides some tools behind other tools. Sometimes finding a tool is difficult, so we created a reference of all the tools and their keystrokes (if available).

The file is called **Photoshop CC 2018 Tools Panel Expanded.pdf**

Keyboard Shortcuts

The filename for the keyboard shortcuts PDF depends on your operating system:

Mac: **Photoshop CC 2018 Shortcuts Mac.pdf**
Windows: **Photoshop CC 2018 Shortcuts Windows.pdf**

Exercise Preview

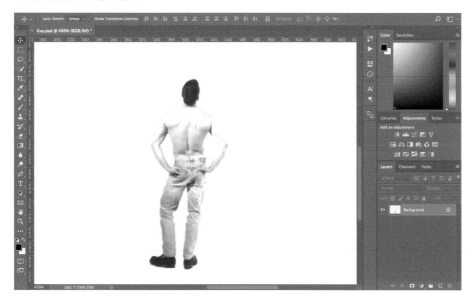

Exercise Overview

In this exercise, you'll start learning the basics of viewing/navigating around images and use some basic Photoshop tools.

Getting Started

1. **Download the class files**. Refer to the **Downloading the Class Files** page at the beginning of the workbook on how to download and install the class files.

2. Launch **Photoshop**.

   NOTE: This book has been tested with **Photoshop CC 2018**.

3. Go to **File > Open**.

4. Navigate to **Desktop > Class Files > Photoshop Class** and double–click on **Guy.psd** to open it.

Restoring Photoshop's Default Settings

1. Let's reset Photoshop's settings, so you have the same settings as this book assumes. Go to **Window > Workspace > Essentials (Default)**.

2. Go to **Window > Workspace > Reset Essentials**.

3. If there is a large **Libraries** panel on the right side of the screen, close it by choosing **Window > Libraries**.

4. **Mac users only**: Go into the **Window** menu. If **Application Frame** is not checked, choose it to turn on the application frame.

5. At the top of the screen is the **Options** bar. As shown below, **Ctrl–click** (Mac) or **Right–click** (Windows) on the leftmost tool icon:

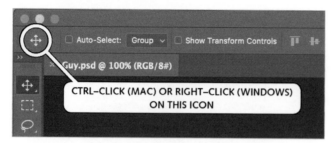

6. From the menu that appears, choose **Reset All Tools**.

7. Click **OK** to confirm.

8. Go into the **Photoshop CC** menu (Mac) or **Edit** menu (Windows) and choose **Preferences > Units & Rulers**.

9. Under **Units**, set the following:

   • Rulers: **Inches**

   • Type: **Points**

10. Click **OK**.

Navigating an Image: Zooming & Scrolling

1. In the **Tools** panel (the toolbox on the left side of the Photoshop window), click on the **Zoom** tool.

2. In the image, position the cursor over the guy's head and click once to zoom in.

3. To zoom back out, hold **Option** (Mac) or **Alt** (Windows) and click once in the image.

4. Let's see a more interactive way to zoom. In the Options bar at the top of the screen, find the **Scrubby Zoom** option.

5. Based on what you see in your Options bar, do the following:

> **If Scrubby Zoom Is Checked On**
>
> 1. Position the cursor over the guy's head.
>
> 2. **Drag right** to zoom **in**.
>
> 3. **Drag left** to zoom **out**.
>
> **If Scrubby Zoom Is Grayed Out (or Unchecked)**
>
> 1. Drag a box over the area you want to see and then release the mouse.
>
>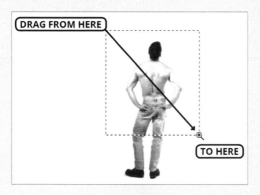

6. To see the whole image again, choose **View > Fit on Screen**.

7. Instead of using the **Zoom** tool, we can also use keystrokes:

   • Zoom **in** by pressing **Cmd–Plus(+)** (Mac) or **Ctrl–Plus(+)** (Windows).

   • Zoom **out** by pressing **Cmd–Minus(-)** (Mac) or **Ctrl–Minus(-)** (Windows).

8. Zoom in a few times so you only see a portion of the image.

9. To scroll around the image, hold the **Spacebar** and drag anywhere on the image. When done, let go of the mouse and the Spacebar.

10. To see the whole image again, choose **View > Fit on Screen**.

Using the Brush Tool

1. In the **Tools** panel, choose the **Brush tool**.

2. At the bottom of the **Tools** panel, click on the **Foreground** color swatch:

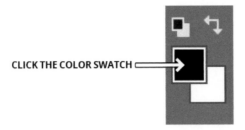

CLICK THE COLOR SWATCH

3. In the window that opens, choose a color as shown below.

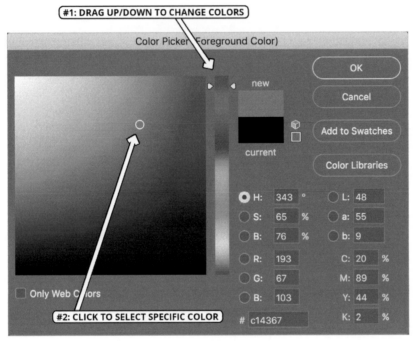

#1: DRAG UP/DOWN TO CHANGE COLORS

Color Picker (Foreground Color)

OK

Cancel

Add to Swatches

Color Libraries

new

current

H:	343	°	L:	48	
S:	65	%	a:	55	
B:	76	%	b:	9	
R:	193		C:	20	%
G:	67		M:	89	%
B:	103		Y:	44	%

Only Web Colors

#2: CLICK TO SELECT SPECIFIC COLOR

c14367

K: 2 %

4. Click **OK**.

5. Drag anywhere on the image to paint with the brush.

6. Let's change the brush color. Towards the bottom of the **Tools** panel, click the **Default Colors** icon to set the Foreground color to black and the Background color to white.

CLICK TO SET DEFAULT COLORS

7. Let's change the brush as well. As shown below, in the **Options** bar at the top of the screen, click on the **Brush Preset picker**.

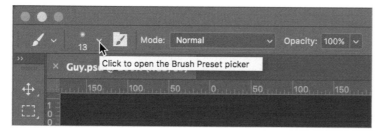

8. Use the sliders to change the **Size** and **Hardness**.

9. Drag anywhere on the image to paint with the new brush.

10. While **Edit > Undo** can undo the very last step, to undo more steps we need to use the **History** panel. Open the **History** panel by going to **Window > History**.

11. Click on the step **before** the **Brush Tool**. This undoes all the brushing.

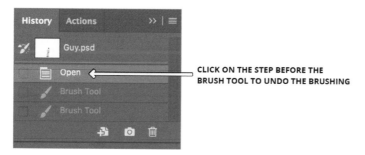

CLICK ON THE STEP BEFORE THE
BRUSH TOOL TO UNDO THE BRUSHING

Basic Selections & Copy/Paste

1. In the **Tools** panel on the left, choose the **Rectangular Marquee** tool ▫.

2. In the image, drag a selection box that encompasses the entire guy.

3. Choose the **Move** tool ✛.

4. Drag anywhere inside the selection and move the guy more to the left.

5. Since the guy is already selected, we'd like to make a copy of him. But before we do, on the right of the screen, look in the **Layers** panel to see that there's only a **Background** layer.

6. Do an **Edit > Copy**.

7. Do an **Edit > Paste**.

8. You won't see major changes in the image, but look in the **Layers** panel on the right to see a new layer named **Layer 1**.

9. Drag the guy to move him. Now you'll be able to see that you are moving the copy!

10. We don't need this copy, so let's delete it. As shown below, in the **Layers** panel, drag **Layer 1** to the **Trash** button 🗑 at the bottom right of the panel.

Using the Clone Stamp Tool

Using the Clone Stamp is like copying and pasting, but on the same layer. In later exercises, you'll come to see it's a powerful retouching tool. Let's see how it works.

1. In the **Tools** panel, choose the **Clone Stamp** tool 🖼.

2. Position the cursor over the thing you want to copy. In this case, the guy's head.

3. **Option–click** (Mac) or **Alt–click** (Windows) to target it as the source area to be copied.

4. If you're still holding Alt/Option, let go of it now.

5. Move the cursor to the white area to the guy's right, where we want to add the cloned area. Notice the cool preview. It's awesome.

6. **Click and drag** with the mouse to paint. The head you targeted in the last step will be cloned here.

7. That's it for our Photoshop warm up. Close the image without saving changes.

Exercise Preview

BEFORE

AFTER

Exercise Overview

In this exercise, you'll perform common retouching tasks: eliminating red eye, erasing facial blemishes, and removing an undesired background element.

1. Go to **File > Open**.

2. Navigate to **Desktop > Class Files > Photoshop Class** and double–click on **WaynesWorld.tif** to open it.

Fixing Blemishes

1. We're going to touch up the blemishes in their faces, so zoom in to get a better look. You can do this by choosing the **Zoom** tool and clicking on the image, or by pressing **Cmd–Plus(+)** (Mac) or **Ctrl–Plus(+)** (Windows).

2. Click and hold on the **Spot Healing Brush** tool and choose the **Healing Brush** tool .

3. We need a small, soft brush, so go to the **Options** bar at the top of the screen and click on the **Brush Preset picker**.

4. In the pop-up panel, set Size to **6 px** and Hardness to **60%**.

5. Close the panel when done.

6. The **Healing Brush** [icon] requires two steps:

   • **Option–click** (Mac) or **Alt–click** (Windows) on a good area of the face to set where you are sampling from.

   • Move the cursor over a blemish and click to fix it.

   HINT: Because you are working with skin textures/tones that change over the face, it's a good idea to **Option–click** (Mac) or **Alt–click** (Windows) fairly close to the blemish so that you get the same general texture/tone.

7. Find another blemish on the faces and repeat the process:

   • **Option–click** (Mac) or **Alt–click** (Windows) on a good area without any facial blemishes.

   • Then click on the blemish (or click and drag to affect a broader area).

   Once you've eliminated a few imperfections, move on to the next step.

8. Choose **View > 100%** to see the best representation of the image's quality for print or web.

9. When you are happy with the image, go into **File > Save As**.

   • From the **Format** (Mac) or **Save as type** (Windows) menu, choose **Photoshop**.

   • If you're not already in the **Photoshop Class** folder, navigate into it.

   • Name the file **yourname-WaynesWorld.psd**

   • Click **Save**.

Removing the Hand

1. To remove Wayne's hand, we must completely cover it over with sky. The **Clone Stamp** tool [icon] is best suited for this, so choose it now.

   NOTE: You use the **Healing Brush** [icon] and **Clone Stamp** [icon] exactly the same way, but the Clone Stamp "clones" an area exactly (almost like copying and pasting), whereas the Healing Brush "heals" an area by melding the textures from the source and the tones from the destination (where you paint).

2. In the **Options** bar at the top of the screen, click on the **Brush Preset picker**.

3. Set the Size to **35 px** and Hardness to **0%**. Close the panel when you're done.

4. **Option–click** (Mac) or **Alt–click** (Windows) in the clouds/sky to define the source that you will be copying. Along the right side, you'll want to sample blue sky. Along the left, you will sample the cloud.

5. Move the cursor over the hand and click and drag on the hand to clone onto that area. Because the background varies in tone, you'll need to **Option–click** (Mac) or **Alt–click** (Windows) in different parts of the clouds/sky to sample different tones to create something that looks natural.

6. As you near the bottom of the hand, you may have to clone over the top edge of Garth's hair to get rid of all of the hand. Don't worry; you will add more hair later.

7. The edge of your cloud may be a bit even and abrupt compared to the original background clouds. To get a varied edge, go to the **Options** bar at the top of the screen and set the Opacity to **20%**.

8. Also in the **Options** bar, click on the **Brush Preset picker** and select a somewhat small, soft-edged brush. (**13 px** with a Hardness of **0%** should be good.)

9. **Option–click** (Mac) or **Alt–click** (Windows) in the cloud to sample from it.

10. Then click along the edge of the cloud to get a bit more variation.

Fixing the Hair

Now that you have covered the hand with sky, the top of Garth's head probably looks a bit rough. Let's patch up the hair with the **Clone Stamp** tool 🔲.

1. Select the **Clone Stamp** 🔲 and in the **Options** bar:

   • Select a small, soft brush (around **10 px** should work).

   • Set the Opacity to **100%**.

2. Look at the top of Garth's head to determine the overall color and direction of the missing hair. **Option–click** (Mac) or **Alt–click** (Windows) on a section of the remaining hair that matches these characteristics.

3. Click and drag along the top of Garth's head to clone over the missing hair.

4. If it doesn't look quite right, try sampling a different area instead:

   • **Option–click** (Mac) or **Alt–click** (Windows) on the hair you like.

   • Then click and drag on the hair you don't like.

   • You'll probably get the best results by sampling several different areas.

Eliminating Red Eye

Finally, it's time to get rid of Wayne's irritating red eye problem. Luckily we have a tool specifically for this.

1. Choose the **Zoom** tool 🔍 and zoom in on Wayne's face.

2. Click and hold on the **Healing Brush** tool ![icon] and choose the **Red Eye** tool ![icon].

   NOTE: If you're using a different workspace, tools may be in different locations.

3. Click once in the red part of Wayne's eye. Voilà! The red eye is gone.

4. Click once on the other eye to fix it.

5. If you want, you can save the file.

   Congratulations—you've completed your first retouching job!

Replacing Backgrounds

Exercise Preview

Exercise Overview

In this exercise, you will combine two separate photos. The first image features a man against a boring background. To make the composition more interesting, you'll cut him out (often called "silhouetting") and place him in front of the second image.

Using the Magic Wand Tool

1. Go to **File > Open**.

2. From the **Photoshop Class** folder, open the files **baseball.jpg** and **security.tif**.

3. Make sure **security.tif** is the active document.

4. From the **Tools** panel, choose the **Magic Wand** tool. If you don't see it, click and hold on the **Quick Selection** tool and then choose it.

   NOTE: The Magic Wand is a selection tool that recognizes color variations. When you click on an area of the image with the Magic Wand, all adjacent areas of similar color will be selected.

5. In the **Options** bar, set the **Tolerance** to **20**. This makes the Magic Wand select fewer colors, therefore less of the image will be selected. Lower numbers equals fewer colors. Higher numbers equals more colors.

6. Click on part of the green background. You'll find that a large part of it becomes selected but that there are many parts of the background that are not yet selected.

7. Go to the **Options** bar at the top of the screen. Near the left, you'll find a row of four similar icons. Currently, the first icon, **New selection** ▣, is highlighted. Click on the second icon, **Add to selection** ▣.

8. Click on another section of the green background. The original selection remains and a new selection is added to it.

9. Continue clicking on the green background until all of it is selected. Don't forget the areas between the railings!

   NOTE: If part of the man or the railings becomes selected, just use **Cmd–Z** (Mac) or **Ctrl–Z** (Windows) to undo your most recent step. Then try clicking on a different section of the background with the **Magic Wand** tool 🪄. You can also change the Tolerance to a lower number to make the Magic Wand pickier.

10. Choose **Select > Inverse**. Instead of having the background selected, you now have everything **except** the background selected.

11. Use **Cmd–C** (Mac) or **Ctrl–C** (Windows) to copy the selected area.

12. Go into the **Window** menu and choose **baseball.jpg** to make it the active document.

13. Use **Cmd–V** (Mac) or **Ctrl–V** (Windows) to paste the copied image onto this image.

14. Go to the **Layers** panel (**Window > Layers**).

    Notice that the content that you've pasted has been automatically placed onto a new layer named **Layer 1**.

15. Double–click directly on the name **Layer 1** and rename it **security**. Hit **Return** (Mac) or **Enter** (Windows) to apply.

16. From the **Tools** panel, choose the **Move** tool ✛.

17. Drag the security guard down or up to line up his bottom edge with the bottom of the document. You will see pink **Smart guides** when it snaps to the bottom. Release the mouse when you see a Smart guide on both the bottom and right sides.

Cleaning Up

1. You may find that tiny bits of the green background show up at some of the guard's edges. Let's fix this.

2. From the **Tools** panel, choose the **Eraser** tool 🩹.

3. In the **Options** bar, choose a fairly small, hard-edged brush. (Try **8 px**.)

4. Use the **Eraser** to carefully brush over the green bits on the edges of the guard's sleeves. (It will help to zoom in for this part.)

   Note that the areas of the security layer that you've erased become transparent.

5. When you're satisfied with the results, do a **File > Save As**.

- Set **Format** (Mac) or **Save as type** (Windows) to **Photoshop**.

- Name it **yourname-baseball.psd** and hit **Save**.

- If it asks you if you want to **Maximize Compatibility**, just leave it checked and click **OK**.

NOTE: Most of the Photoshop class files have been saved as JPEG documents to conserve file size, but you'll always want to save the master copy of your image as a Photoshop Document (.psd). This ensures that the image retains the maximum amount of editability, such as multiple layers. It also maintains the image's quality. JPEG compression reduces the image quality in order to make the file smaller.

To Maximize or Not to Maximize?

When saving a Photoshop file (.psd) you may see a dialog with an option to **Maximize Compatibility**. We recommend keeping Maximize Compatibility turned on, so feel free to check on **Don't show again** so you won't be nagged by this option every time you save. If you want to know what this option does, read the following comparison.

Maximize Compatibility ON
- The document will be more compatible with older versions of Photoshop.

- You should maximize compatibility if working with Adobe InDesign.

- The file size may be larger.

Maximize Compatibility OFF
- The document won't be as compatible with older versions of Photoshop.

- The file size may be smaller.

Exercise Preview

Exercise Overview

This exercise will give you practice making selections, feathering selections, copying from file to file, adding type, and using layer opacity.

1. In Photoshop, close any files you have open.

2. In the **Photoshop Class** folder, open the file **Report Cover.jpg**.

3. To enlarge the image on-screen so it will be easy to do the fine selection work we're about to do, go to **View > Fit on Screen**.

4. As shown below, in the **Layers** panel, click and drag the **Background** layer down to the **New layer** icon 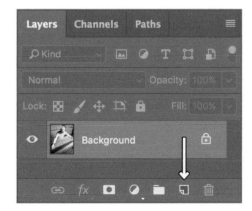 at the bottom right. This creates a duplicate layer that we can edit without changing the original image.

Desaturating the Background to Make the Pasta "Pop"

1. Click on the **Polygonal Lasso** tool ⬚. If you don't see it, click and hold on the **Lasso** tool ⬚ and then choose it.

2. Click on a corner of the tray of spaghetti between the man's arms, then move to another corner and click again. Continue clicking on corners until you've returned to your first corner. Click on that corner or hit **Return** (Mac) or **Enter** (Windows) to complete the pasta selection.

3. Once you have the whole tray selected, go into **Select > Modify > Feather**.

4. Set the **Feather Radius** to **2** pixels and click **OK**. This softens the edge of the selection slightly so our adjustment will blend at the edge.

5. Go to the **Select** menu and choose **Inverse**.

6. Go into **Image > Adjustments > Hue/Saturation**.

   • Change the **Saturation** by typing **–75** in its field (that's negative 75!).

   • Change the **Lightness** by typing **25** in its field.

7. Click **OK**.

8. Deselect the selection using **Cmd–D** (Mac) or **Ctrl–D** (Windows).

Adding a Soft Oval Frame

1. If the rulers are not already showing, go into the **View** menu and select **Rulers**.

2. If the rulers aren't in inches, **Ctrl–click** (Mac) or **Right–click** (Windows) in the ruler and choose **Inches** from the menu.

3. Go to **View > 100%**. The rulers should now have a tick mark every 0.125" ($\frac{1}{8}$"). If it doesn't, you'll probably need to zoom in more (using **Cmd–Plus(+)** (Mac) or **Ctrl–Plus(+)** (Windows)).

4. Go to the **View** menu, and make sure that **Snap** is checked.

5. Select the **Move** tool ✛.

6. Position the mouse over the left ruler. You are going to pull a guide out by clicking and dragging from the ruler. Hold **Shift** (to make the guides snap into place at the tick), then click and drag the mouse so that a guide is positioned **0.375"** inside the left edge. (That's three ruler tick marks from the edge.)

   NOTE: To move a guide after it is set into place, you must use the **Move** tool ✛.

7. Pull another guide down from the top ruler. Position it **0.375"** inside the top edge.

8. Pull out two more guides so that they are **0.375"** from the right and bottom edges.

9. Choose the **Elliptical Marquee** tool ⬭ (if you don't see it, click and hold on the **Rectangular Marquee** tool ⬚, then choose it).

10. Position the mouse at the intersection of the top and left guides.

11. Click and drag to the intersection of the guides at the bottom right of the image to draw an oval selection.

    NOTE: If we hadn't set **Snap**, it would've been much harder to get the ellipse sized and positioned correctly. With **Snap**, it snaps to the guides.

12. In the **Options** bar at the top of the screen, click the **Select and Mask** button. (Prior to CC 2015.5 this was called **Refine Edge**.)

13. In the **Properties** panel on the right:

    • Click on the thumbnail to the right of **View** and double–click **On White**.

    • Set **Opacity** to **100%**.

    • In the **Global Refinements** section, change **Feather** to **15 px**.

    • You should see a preview of this feathered edge on a white background.

    • In the **Output Settings** section, make sure **Output To** is set to **Selection**.

    • Click **OK**.

14. The selection now appears as a line of "marching ants," as they are often called. Even though it may not look like it, don't worry; the selection is still feathered.

15. From the **Select** menu, choose **Inverse**.

16. If it isn't already showing, open the **Layers** panel (**Window > Layers**).

17. To fill the oval frame, we'll use a fill layer because its color can later be easily changed. As shown below, at the bottom of the **Layers** panel, click the **Create new fill or adjustment layer** button ◑ and from the menu, choose **Solid Color**.

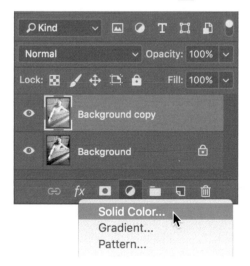

18. In the Color Picker that appears, choose **white** and click **OK**.

19. Double–click directly on the layer's name and rename it **Oval Frame**. Hit **Return** (Mac) or **Enter** (Windows) to apply.

20. Hide the guides from view by choosing **View > Show > Guides**.

Adding the Pepper Picture

1. From the **Photoshop Class** folder, open the **Red Pepper.psd** file.

2. Choose the **Move** tool ⊕.

3. In the **Layers** panel, double–click directly on the name **Background**. Rename it **Pepper** and hit **Return** (Mac) or **Enter** (Windows).

4. To copy the peppers into the Report Cover file, do the following:

   • With the Pepper layer still selected, do an **Edit > Copy**. If Copy is grayed out, refer to the sidebar below.

   • Switch back to the design file **Report Cover.jpg** using the tab at the top.

   • Go to **Edit > Paste**.

> ### In Photoshop CC 2017 & Older
>
> CC 2018 made moving layers between files as easy as copy and paste. Previously it was a bit less intuitive. Here's how we used to do it:
>
> 1. Make sure both files are open (the file that contains the layer you want to copy and the file you want to put it in).
>
> 2. In the **Layers** panel, **Ctrl–click** (Mac) or **Right–click** (Windows) on the name of the layer you want to move/copy and choose **Duplicate Layers** from the menu that appears.
>
> 3. Set the Destination **Document** to the file you want to move the layer into. (Next to **As**, change the layer name if desired.)
>
> 4. Click **OK**.

5. Look in the **Layers** panel and notice that a new layer named **Pepper** has been created.

6. Use the **Move** tool ⊕ to bring the image to the lower-right corner. It should snap into place and you should see the pink Smart guides when you get close. Otherwise, you can use the Arrow keys to fine-tune the placement.

7. The pepper image would stand out better if it had a thin black line around it. At the bottom of the **Layers** panel, click the **Add a layer style** button 𝑓𝑥 and from the menu, choose **Stroke**.

8. Set the following options:

   Size: **2 px**

   Position: **Inside**

   Blend Mode: **Normal**

   Opacity: **100%**

   Overprint: Make sure it is **unchecked**

   Fill Type: **Color**

   Color: Click on the color swatch next to **Color**. In the Color Picker that appears, choose **black** in the bottom-right corner.

9. When done, click **OK**.

Adding the Type

1. Choose the **Horizontal Type** tool T .

2. In the **Options** bar at the top of the screen, click the **Color** swatch.

CLICK HERE

3. Move the dialog that appears so you can see the red pepper. Mouse over the pepper and notice that the cursor turns into the **Eyedropper** tool 🖋 . Click with the **Eyedropper** 🖋 to sample the red from the pepper.

4. Click **OK**.

5. You will be back in the **Horizontal Type** tool T . Position the cursor somewhere near the top left-hand corner, then click.

6. Type in the words **Annual Report**.

7. Highlight the text and in the **Options** bar at the top of the screen, set:

   Font: **Times Bold** (or something similar)

   Font Size ⬚T : **20 pt** (Type in the number.)

   Anti-Aliasing aₐ : **Crisp**

8. In order to track out the letters, you must open the **Character** panel. You can choose **Window > Character** or click the **Panels** button ▤ on the right of the **Options** bar.

9. Set the **Tracking** VA to **140**.

10. When done with the type, click the **checkbox** ✓ toward the right side of the **Options** bar. (If it's not there, don't worry—Photoshop already automatically applied the changes for you.)

11. In the **Layers** panel, you should now see a layer named **Annual Report**. This layer has a **T** thumbnail image T to indicate that it is a type layer.

12. Select the **Move** tool ✛ and move the type so it starts about ¼" from the top and about ⅛" from the left.

13. Choose the **Horizontal Type** tool T again.

14. Click in the center of the image and type **2018** (or the current year).

15. Highlight the text and make it:

    > Font: **Times Italic** (or something similar)

    Font Size T: **120 pt**

16. In the **Character** panel (**Window > Character**):

    • Click the swatch next to **Color** and in the window that appears, choose **black** then click **OK**.

    • Set the **Tracking** VA to **0**.

17. Using the **Move** tool ✛, position the type so it's nicely centered on the image.

18. Notice that in the **Layers** panel, a new type layer named **2018** (or the current year) is highlighted. Above the layer name, near the top of the panel, is the **Opacity** of that layer. Change it to **40%**.

19. Do a **File > Save As**.

20. Set **Format** (Mac) or **Save as type** (Windows) to **Photoshop**.

21. Name the file **yourname-Report Cover.psd** and click **Save**.

    NOTE: Saving as a Photoshop document (.psd) file will save all layers and editable items like type.

Exercise Preview

Exercise Overview

Often, selecting part of an image proves too intricate for conventional selection tools. Quick Mask Mode allows you to use painting tools to create or refine selections, allowing for greater precision.

Starting the Selection Using Traditional Selection Tools

1. From the **Photoshop Class** folder, open the file **watchingSailboat.tif**.

2. Choose the **Magic Wand** tool .

3. In the **Options** bar:

   • Set the **Tolerance** to **32** (this is the Magic Wand's default setting).

   • Click **Add to selection** .

4. Click on part of the water and trees around the man and girl.

5. Continue clicking on the area around the man and girl until most of it is selected.

   • Focus on getting the best selection you can around the man and girl. But don't worry if it's not perfect—we'll be finishing it in the following steps.

   • It's OK if you miss a few spots in the background. That's easy to fix later.

6. Go to **Select > Inverse** so the people are selected rather than the surrounding area.

Refining the Selection in Quick Mask Mode

1. As shown, in the **Tools** panel, there's an **Edit in Quick Mask Mode** button .

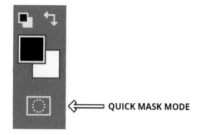

⇐ **QUICK MASK MODE**

2. Double–click the **Quick Mask Mode** button to set its display options.

3. In the dialog that opens, choose Color Indicates: **Selected Areas** and click **OK**.

   NOTE: You're now in Quick Mask Mode, where your selection is indicated by colored shading instead of the marching ants dotted outline. In this mode, we can change the selection by painting with **black** to **select** and painting with **white** to **deselect**. You won't see black and white as you paint, though. Painting with **black** should appear as **red** unless the color was changed in the Quick Mask Options dialog you were just in. Painting with **white** would remove the color, indicating the area will be **deselected**.

   We want to **add** to our selection, so we need to be painting with **black**.

4. As shown below, in the **Tools** panel, click the **Default Colors** icon to make sure the **Foreground** color is pure **black**.

CLICK TO SET DEFAULT COLORS ⟹

5. Choose the **Brush** tool and in the **Options** bar:

   • Pick a **large**, **hard-edged** brush.

   • Set the Opacity and Flow to **100%**.

6. Most of the man and girl are shaded already, but you may have missed some pieces:

   • Completely shade in the large solid areas of the man and girl. We'll get to the edge details in a few steps.

   • Don't worry about the background for now.

   NOTE: You're painting with **black**, which adds shading, therefore **selecting** them.

7. Press the **X** key on your keyboard to swap the **Foreground** and **Background** colors.

8. You're now painting with **white**, which removes shading, therefore **deselecting**. Paint over any areas of the background to remove the colored shading.

9. Check the other edges of the man and the girl. Where necessary:

   • Paint with **white** to **deselect** (remove the shading).

   • Paint with **black** to **select** (add shading).

   • Soft brushes may work better for hair edges, but you'll probably want hard brushes for everything else.

   • To create a feathered look for the wispy hair, you may want to reduce the opacity of your brush in the **Options** bar.

10. You should now be finished painting the selection. In the **Tools** panel, click the **Edit in Standard Mode** button 🔲 shown below.

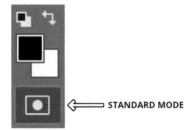

◁━━━━ STANDARD MODE

11. Notice that the shading became a selection. Neat!

12. Double-check the selection for little spots you may have missed (the "marching ants" at selection edges should make it obvious). If you've missed an area, go back into **Quick Mask Mode** to correct it, then return to **Standard Mode**.

    NOTE: Quick Mask Mode is only for making selections and will not allow you to edit the image at all. Always return to **Standard Mode** when you've finished making a selection in **Quick Mask Mode**.

Putting the People onto a New Background

1. Go to **Select > Modify > Contract**.

2. Enter a value of **1** and click **OK**.

   By using Contract, we moved the edges of our selection in by one pixel, cleaning up our selection a bit.

3. Use **Cmd–C** (Mac) or **Ctrl–C** (Windows) to copy the selected area.

4. Go to **File > Open**, and from the **Photoshop Class** folder, open **shore.tif**.

5. Use **Cmd–V** (Mac) or **Ctrl–V** (Windows) to paste the copied image onto this image.

6. Use the **Move** tool ⊕ to position them in the new picture.

   This looks a little awkward since the light on the people is from the left, but the light on the landscape is from the right.

7. Go to **Edit > Transform > Flip Horizontal**.

8. Reposition them on the left of the image as needed.

   Much better! Now the light sources match fairly well and the people have a crisp, precise silhouette, thanks to Quick Mask Mode!

9. If you like, save the file as **yourname-watching the shore.psd**

Exercise Preview

Exercise Overview

This exercise shows you the basics of using layers and how to create drop shadows.

Silhouetting the Turtle

1. From the **Photoshop Class** folder, open the **Turtle.jpg** file.

2. Choose the **Magic Wand** tool.

3. In the **Options** bar, make sure:

    • The **New selection** icon is clicked.

    • **Tolerance** is **32**.

    • **Anti-alias** and **Contiguous** are checked.

4. Click on the white background.

5. Turn the selection inside-out by using **Select > Inverse**.

    We're going to use a **Layer Effect** to create a drop shadow. The Drop Shadow effect is found in the **Layer** menu, under **Layer Style**. However, you can't access the menu now, because we are currently working on the **Background** layer. Photoshop can not put a shadow on a **Background** layer.

6. To separate the turtle from the Background layer, do a **Layer > New > Layer Via Cut**.

7. The turtle is now on its own layer, ready for the Drop Shadow. In the **Layers** panel, double–click the layer's name and rename it **turtle**.

Adding the Drop Shadow

As previously mentioned, you can add a drop shadow by choosing it from the **Layer** menu, but let's do it an easier way.

1. At the bottom of the **Layers** panel, click the **Add a layer style** button _fx_ and from the menu, choose **Drop Shadow**, as shown below.

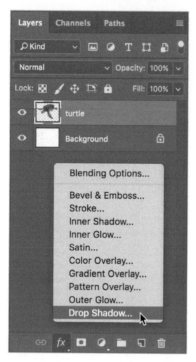

2. When the dialog opens, you will notice a little shadow underneath the turtle. Try moving it around by clicking inside the image window and dragging it around.

3. Set the following options in the **Layer Style** dialog:

   Blend Mode: **Multiply**

   Opacity: **50%**

   Angle: This one's up to you! (Distance and Angle are determined when you drag the shadow in the window.)

   Distance: Also up to you!

   Spread: **0%**

   Size: **8 px**

   Noise: **0%**

4. Click **OK**.

5. That's how easy it is to create a drop shadow! Look in the **Layers** panel. To the right of the **turtle** layer, there is an effects icon *fx*, which indicates there is a layer style. Below the **turtle** layer, the **Effects** are listed.

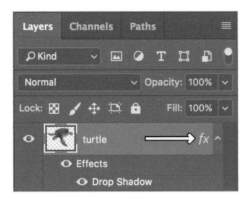

6. To clean up the **Layers** panel, click the up arrow ⌃ just to the right of this symbol. Notice how the Drop Shadow listing is hidden.

7. Click the arrow again, and you can see the list of **Effects** once again.

8. If you double–click on the name of the effect, you will be able to alter the shadow's settings like distance, light angle, opacity, etc. Try it out for fun.

Moving the Turtle onto Another Picture

1. Open **water.psd**. We want to make this the new background for the turtle.

2. Switch back to **turtle.jpg** using the tab at the top. Then do the following to copy its **turtle** layer (make sure it's still selected):

   • Do an **Edit > Copy**. If Copy is grayed out, refer to the sidebar below.

   • Return to **water.psd**.

   • Go to **Edit > Paste**.

In Photoshop CC 2017 & Older

1. Make sure both files are open (the file that contains the layer you want to copy and the file you want to put it in).

2. In the **Layers** panel, **Ctrl–click** (Mac) or **Right–click** (Windows) on the name of the layer you want to move/copy and choose **Duplicate Layers** from the menu that appears.

3. Set the Destination **Document** to the file you want to move the layer into. (Next to **As**, change the layer name if desired.) When done, click **OK**.

---

3. Look in the **Layers** panel and notice that the **turtle** layer (the turtle and its shadow) go copied into this document.

4. Close the **Turtle.jpg** file and don't bother saving changes.

5. The **water.psd** document is now active, so you can move the turtle around. Notice that the shadow is still there, moving with the layer! If the shadow is not in the same position as it was in **Turtle.jpg**, double–click on the **Drop Shadow** effect and uncheck **Use Global Light**.

6. Move the turtle so he's nicely centered in the water.

7. Let's make it look like he's underwater. Go to the **Layers** panel and make sure the **turtle** layer is highlighted.

8. Change the **Opacity** to around **30%** or whatever you think looks realistic.

9. It looks like he's underwater but his shadow doesn't look right. Double–click the turtle's **Drop Shadow** effect. Adjust the Angle, Size, and Opacity to make it look like the shadow is hitting the ocean floor.

10. If you want to save this, choose **File > Save As** and:

    • Make sure **Format** (Mac) or **Save as type** (Windows) is set to **Photoshop**.

    • Name the file **yourname-dropshadow-layered.psd** and click **Save**.

    NOTE: Remember that a .psd is a fully editable layered document that you can make changes to later on. If you're taking this image into InDesign, you don't have to do anything else, as InDesign can import/print the .psd file. For further explanation, refer to the **Print File Formats** reference at the back of this workbook.

Exercise Preview

Exercise Overview

Regular drop shadows are only 2D, but in this exercise, you'll learn how to make them look 3D!

Adding 2D Drop Shadow to Text

1. From the **Photoshop Class** folder, open the file **italy.psd**.

2. Choose the **Horizontal Type** tool ![T].

3. In the **Options** bar at the top of the screen, make the text **Arial Black**, **100 pt**, and **Center text** ![icon].

4. Click in the middle of the street (on the lane divider line) and type the word **ITALY** in all caps.

5. While still in the **Horizontal Type** tool ![T], select the text and go into the **Character** panel (**Window > Character**).

6. Click the **Color** swatch and in the window that appears, choose **black**.

7. From the **Kerning** menu ![VA], choose **Optical**. Ahh, now the text looks better.

8. Choose the **Move** tool ![icon] and position the text in the middle of the road, making sure to leave enough space below it for the shadow.

9. In the **Layers** panel (**Window > Layers**), make sure the ITALY layer is still selected.

10. At the bottom of the **Layers** panel, click **Add a layer style** *fx* and from the menu, choose **Drop Shadow**. Set the following options before clicking **OK**:

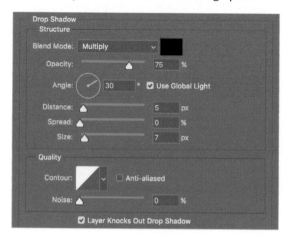

Using Transform to Create a 3D Effect

1. In order to transform the shadow, we need to break it off into a separate layer. Go into **Layer > Layer Style > Create Layer**. A warning may appear telling you that some layer effects can't be reproduced with layers. It doesn't affect us, so click **OK**.

2. Click on the new layer **ITALY's Drop Shadow** and go to **Edit > Transform > Distort**.

3. Distort the text so it looks like the finished product. Use the pictures below as a guide. Hit **Return** (Mac) or **Enter** (Windows) when you're happy with the results.

4. Use the **Move** tool ⊕ to move the shadow up a bit so it's touching the bottom edge of the text.

5. If you think the shape still needs more fine-tuning:

   • Go back to **Edit > Transform > Distort**.

   • In the **Layers** panel, reduce the **Opacity** as desired. Ciao!

Exercise Preview

Organic Camel Milk at a Grocery Store Near You!

Exercise Overview

When text is placed over a photo or a pattern, it can be difficult to read.
The technique we'll teach you in this exercise can help!

Adding the Text Layer

1. From the **Photoshop Class** folder, open the file **camel.tif**.

2. Make sure that you can see the entire image.

3. Press **D** to make sure you have the default foreground and background colors.

4. If the rulers are not already showing, go into the **View** menu and select **Rulers**.

5. Use the **Rectangular Marquee** tool to draw a selection over the bottom half inch, across the entire image. Use the Rulers to guide you.

6. Go to the **Layers** panel (**Window > Layers**).

7. At the bottom of the **Layers** panel, click the **Create new fill or adjustment layer** button, and from the menu, choose **Solid Color**.

8. In the Color Picker that appears, choose **white** and click **OK**.

9. Double–click the layer's name and rename it **ghosted color**.

10. At the top of the **Layers** panel, adjust the opacity of the **ghosted color** layer. Try **50%** first, then experiment.

    TIP: When the mouse is over the word Opacity, it will turn into a hand slider 👆. Just click and drag left or right to quickly adjust the value.

11. Choose the **Horizontal Type** tool T .

12. In the **Options** bar at the top of the screen, make the text **Myriad Pro Bold**, **14 pt**, and **Left aligned** .

13. Click once in the far left of the ghosted color area so you have a blinking text cursor.

14. Type in the following: **Organic Camel Milk at a Grocery Store Near You!**

15. Choose the **Move** tool .

16. Use the **Arrow keys** to nudge the text into the center of the white ghosted box.

    TIP: Pressing **Shift–Arrow key** moves **10 px** at a time to make it faster.

Feathering the Layer to Add More Subtlety

The hard top edge of the ghosted white box is a little abrupt. Let's soften it.

1. In the **Layers** panel, select the layer mask in the **ghosted color** layer as shown below:

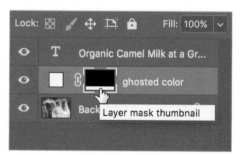

2. In the **Properties** panel (**Window > Properties**), set the **Feather** to **20 px**.

3. If you don't like the look of the soft edge and prefer the hard edge, just set it back to **0 px** or whatever you think looks good.

   The nice thing about feathering the mask in this way is that it is non-destructive so you can change it anytime you want.

4. Do a **File > Save As**, make sure **Format** (Mac) or **Save as type** (Windows) is set to **Photoshop**, and name the file **yourname-camel.psd**

Exercise Preview

Exercise Overview

The opacity of a layer's contents and effects can be controlled separately to create dynamic results. Let's see how in this graphic for Saturday Night Live (SNL).

Setting Up the Type Layer

1. From the **Photoshop Class** folder, open the file **nyc at night.jpg**.

2. At the bottom of the **Tools** panel, click on the **Foreground** color swatch.

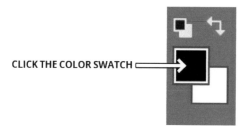

CLICK THE COLOR SWATCH

3. In the color picker that appears, choose **white** and click **OK**.

4. Choose the **Horizontal Type** tool T.

5. In the Options bar at the top of the screen, set the text formatting to **Myriad Pro Bold** and **135 pt**.

6. Click in the center of the image.

7. Type: **SNL**

8. Choose the **Move** tool ⊕.

9. Position the text in the lower-left corner so the Chrysler Building sits between the S and N.

Adding Effects & Adjusting Layer Fill

1. At the bottom of the **Layers** panel, click the **Add a layer style** button *fx* and from the menu, choose **Outer Glow**.

2. Set the following:

   Spread: **6%**
       Size: **50 px**

3. Click **OK**.

4. Near the top right of the **Layers** panel, adjust the **Fill** (%) of the layer. Try **15%** first. Then just experiment.

   TIP: When the mouse is over the word **Fill**, it will turn into a hand slider 🖑. Click and drag left or right to quickly adjust the value.

5. Notice how the white text fill is partially transparent, but the effect wasn't altered? When you are satisfied, **File > Save As** a **Photoshop** document. Name the file **yourname-nyc at night.psd**

Fill vs. Opacity

While Fill and Opacity are similar, think of them this way:

Opacity: Affects transparency of layer contents AND effects

Fill: Affects transparency of layer contents, NOT effects

Exercise Overview

We have a collection of files from a photo shoot. We need to choose our top picks to present to a client. Adobe Bridge is a program that comes with Photoshop and will help us in our project.

Navigating to a Folder

1. Launch **Adobe Bridge** using one of these two ways:

   • Directly launch **Bridge**.

   • In any Creative Cloud program (such as Photoshop), choose **File > Browse in Bridge**.

2. To make sure we're looking at the same thing:

   • Go to **Window > Workspace > Essentials**.

   • Then go to **Window > Workspace > Reset Workspace**.

3. At the top left of the window, you should see a **Favorites** and a **Folders** tab.

4. You should already be viewing the **Favorites** tab, so in the list of favorites click on **Desktop**.

5. The icons are fairly small. To make it easier to read longer names, let's make the icons bigger. At the bottom right of the window, drag the zoom slider (illustrated below) a little to the right.

6. In the middle section of the window, find the **Class Files** folder and double–click it to open it.

7. Double–click on the **Photoshop Class** folder.

8. Double–click on the **Collection of Files** folder (NOT the **Collections** tab you may see on the left). If you don't see the folder, you may need to scroll to find it.

9. Now that you see the collection of files, play with the zoom slider to see how the thumbnail sizes change.

Organizing Some of the Files

1. Go to **View > Sort > By Filename** to properly order the files.

2. Make sure **View > Sort > Ascending Order** is checked so the files you are looking at are sorted in A–Z order.

3. Several of these files belong to the same project. It would be nice to put them all together in a folder. Go to **File > New Folder**.

4. Name the new folder **Australia Ad**.

5. Click once on the thumbnail of the InDesign file named **australia ad-started.indd**.

6. Hold **Shift** and click on the thumbnail of the Illustrator file named **australia dot com logo-white.ai**.

   All four Australia files should now be selected: one InDesign layout, one text file, and two logos.

7. Drag any of the selected thumbnails into the **Australia Ad** folder.

8. Double–click on the **Australia Ad** folder to go into it. The files are there!

9. At the top of the window, notice that the file path is displayed. Click on the **Collection of Files** folder to go back to it (you can click the folder or the name).

CLICK HERE

Rotating Images

1. Some of the images need to be rotated. Click once on the image named **_MG_0134.jpg**. (It's one of the night shots.)

2. Hold **Shift** and click on the image named **_MG_0136.jpg**. The image in between should have been selected as well. **Three** images should now be selected.

   NOTE: To select images that are not in a continuous row, you can hold **Cmd** (Mac) or **Ctrl** (Windows) when clicking on the images.

3. To rotate the images, press **Cmd–]** (Mac) or **Ctrl–]** (Windows).

Deleting the Worst Images

1. Some of the images are too bad to even keep. To judge them better, we want to see larger previews. Go to **Window > Workspace > Preview**.

2. To make sure we're seeing the same thing, go to **Window > Workspace > Reset Workspace**.

3. Flip between images by clicking on a thumbnail or hitting the **Up/Down Arrows**.

4. Arrow up/down to (or click on) the **fourth** image (**_MG_0132.jpg**), which is a picture of a fence with the Chrysler building in the distance.

5. Hit the **Down Arrow** to see the next picture, which is very similar, but the background is more out of focus.

6. Flip between these two images a couple of times by hitting the **Up/Down Arrows** to quickly compare the differences between the images.

7. We don't like the second, more blurry image so we can delete it. With that image selected (**_MG_0133.jpg**), hit **Delete**.

8. A message will probably ask if you want to reject or delete the file. Click **Delete**.

9. You may also be asked to confirm the deletion. Just click **OK**.

   NOTE: In the future, it's easier to hit **Cmd–Delete** (Mac) or **Ctrl–Delete** (Windows).

Renaming Images

1. At the top of the window, click the **Essentials** button to switch back to that view.

2. Adjust the thumbnail size so you can nicely see all the images by dragging the slider at the bottom right of the window.

3. We want to rename the **third** image **_MG_0113.jpg**. Click on it once to select it.

4. Click directly on the filename (not the thumbnail), and after a moment the name will become editable.

5. Type in the new filename: **noble desktop** (leave the **.jpg** after the name).

6. Select the **Sydney Opera House** image (named **2005-10-08 20-56-23.jpg**).

7. Click on the filename and after a moment you can type in the new filename: **sydney opera house** (leaving the **.jpg** after the name).

8. Click on the thumbnail of the first image **_MG_0075.jpg** to select it.

9. Hold **Shift** and click on the second image **_MG_0076.jpg** so both images are selected.

10. Go to **Tools > Batch Rename**.

    A Batch Rename dialog appears. Don't click Rename until we say so!

11. Under **Destination Folder**, leave **Rename in same folder** selected.

12. Under **New Filenames**, go into the leftmost top menu and choose **Text**.

13. To its right, type in **grand central** (and type a **space** at the end).

14. If there's not a second row of options below, click the **plus** button ⊕ to the right.

15. In the second row, from the left-hand menu, choose **Sequence Number**.

16. Make sure the **Sequence Number** is set to **1**.

17. Make sure the menu to the right of **Sequence Number** says **One Digit**.

18. If there's a third row or more, click the **minus** button ⊖ to the right of each row and remove all additional rows.

19. Click **Rename**.

20. Click on the first **koala** picture.

21. Hold **Shift** and click on the last **koala** image.

22. Go to **Tools > Batch Rename**.

23. Most of the previous options are correct, but change the text to **koala** (with a **space** at the end).

24. Make sure **Sequence Number** is set to **1**.

25. Click **Rename**.

26. We're done with Bridge, so quit out of it:

    Mac: Go to **Adobe Bridge CC 2018 > Quit Adobe Bridge CC 2018**.
    Windows: Go to **File > Exit**.

27. Go back to Photoshop. And that's how Adobe Bridge complements your workflow!

Exercise Preview

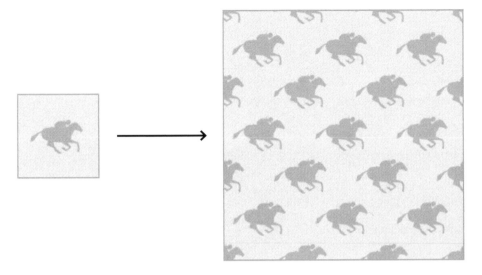

Exercise Overview

Repeating patterns can be useful for creating a wallpapered or textured look in an image. In this exercise, we'll look at how to create patterns in Photoshop.

Working with Basic Patterns

1. From the **Photoshop Class** folder, open **patterns.psd**.

2. Make sure the **Layers** panel is open. The **pawprint** layer should be visible.

3. Go to **Select > All**.

4. Go to **Edit > Define Pattern**.

5. In the dialog that appears, name the pattern **yourname-pawprint** and click **OK**.

   That's it! You've created a pattern. Let's test out how it looks as it repeats by filling a separate file with the pattern.

6. Go to **File > New** and on the right under **Preset Details** set the following:

   Width: **400 px**
   Height: **400 px**
   Resolution: **72 Pixels/Inch** (ppi)
   Color Mode: **RGB Color**
   Background Contents: **White**

7. Uncheck **Artboards**.

8. Click **Create**.

9. In the **Layers** panel, click the **Create new fill or adjustment layer** button and choose **Pattern**.

   It should come up with the pattern you just created, so click **OK**. If it wasn't chosen, click the pattern thumbnail and choose it. (It will be at the end of the list.)

10. This image repeats just fine, but perhaps we'd rather have the paws more tightly spaced. Leave this file open and switch back to the **patterns.psd** file.

11. Go to **Select > Deselect**.

12. Choose the **Rectangular Marquee** tool . In the **Options** bar, make sure **Feather** is set to **0** pixels.

13. Draw a selection around the paw. Leave only a little bit of extra space around it.

14. Go into **Edit > Define Pattern**.

15. In the dialog that appears, name the pattern **yourname-pawprint2** and click **OK**.

16. Switch back to the test file (it's probably called **Untitled-1**).

17. In the **Layers** panel, double–click on the icon for the **Pattern Fill 1** layer . Find the new pattern by clicking on the pattern thumbnail and choosing **yourname-pawprint2** (it will be at the end of the list).

   Check it out! Now **yourname-pawprint2** contains less of the light area around the paw, so in the tiled result, the paws are more tightly spaced.

18. If you haven't already, click **OK** to exit the **Pattern Fill** dialog.

Offsetting to Create Complex Patterns

1. Switch back to the **patterns.psd** file.

2. Click the **eye** beside the **pawprint** layer to hide that layer.

3. As shown below, click on the **Horse** layer to highlight it and make it visible by clicking in the empty box where the **eye** should be.

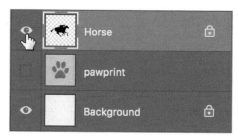

4. Go to **Select > All** then **Edit > Define Pattern**.

5. In the dialog that appears, name the pattern **yourname-horse** and click **OK**.

6. Switch back to the test file (it's probably called **Untitled-1**).

7. In the **Layers** panel, double–click on the icon for the **Pattern Fill 1** layer ▣.

   Switch it to display the horse pattern.

8. Observe the results. It's OK, but with boring, obviously grid-like repetition. Let's switch back to the **patterns.psd** file.

9. Duplicate the **Horse** layer by dragging the layer onto the **New layer** button 🖫 at the bottom of the panel.

10. Make sure the copy is highlighted, then go into **Filter > Other > Offset**. Do not click **OK** until we tell you.

11. In the dialog that opens, set the following:

    Horizontal pixels right: **50 px**
    Vertical pixels down: **50 px**
    Wrap Around: Make sure it is **selected**

12. Click **OK**.

    NOTE: We're using 50 px because it is half of the whole document, which is 100 x 100 pixels.

13. Look at the document. You see that it has split the horse and placed it in the corners. The Offset filter simply moved the pixels 50 to the right and 50 down. If any pixels went off the canvas, they wrapped around to the other side. So really we're just shifting pixels here.

14. Do a **Select > All** and **Edit > Define Pattern** again.

15. This time, name the pattern **yourname-horse2** and click **OK**.

16. Switch to the test document.

17. Double–click on the icon for the **Pattern Fill 1** layer 🖵.

18. Choose the new pattern you just created (it will be at the end of the list).

19. Click **OK**.

    This tiled background is more interesting, and less predictably grid-like!

20. Experiment with the other layers in the **patterns.psd** document:

    - With the **Swirl** layer, don't duplicate the layer. Simply do an Offset, then draw your own art inside the open space to fill in the gaps.

    - With the **leaves** layer, just run the Offset filter and then use the **Clone Stamp** or **Healing Brush** on the edges inside to make the seams invisible. (It may help to use a soft-edged brush.)

    NOTE: Sometimes when you are working with an image, some pixels get stored off of the canvas. That means they are there, but you just can't see them. This is why sometimes you can move something off the canvas, then drag it back in. If you do have any pixels off the canvas, then Offset will also move those pixels, and you may get problematic results. The solution to this problem, if it happens to you: Take the **Crop** tool, outline the canvas, and in the **Options** bar make sure **Delete Cropped Pixels** is checked. Then hit **Return** (Mac) or **Enter** (Windows) to crop the image to the exact canvas size.

Deleting & Resetting Patterns

Photoshop saves all the patterns that you create. Eventually you may end up with a lot of them in your patterns window. What if you want to get rid of one or all of them?

- Go into **Edit > Presets > Preset Manager**.

- Under **Preset Type**, choose **Patterns**.

- Select the pattern(s) you want to delete.

- Click **Delete**.

- To reset all the patterns back to factory standard, click on the **options menu** near the top right, choose **Reset Patterns** and click **OK**. If it asks you if you want to save changes, click **Don't Save** (Mac) or **No** (Windows). This will delete all custom patterns and revert back to the default ones.

Exercise Preview

Exercise Overview

This exercise shows you the Gradient tool and how to apply fills with special blending options such as "Multiply." It also reviews selections and patterns.

Cleaning Up the Background

1. From the **Photoshop Class** folder, open **Riddick Bowe.tif**.

2. Select the **Crop** tool 🔲.

3. Notice how the whole image is selected, with handles in all four corners and on all four sides. Simply drag the handle on the right to crop out the **BUDW sign**. You can also click and drag in the middle to move the whole cropping area.

4. Once the crop is placed correctly, do any **one** of the following:

   • Click the **checkbox** ✅ at the right in the **Options** bar.

   • Hit **Return** (Mac) or **Enter** (Windows).

   • Double–click inside the cropped area.

5. The tone of the black background around Riddick currently varies slightly, and it's not a truly solid black. Select the **Magic Wand** tool 🪄 so we can change that.

6. In the **Options** bar, set the tolerance to **20** and make sure **Contiguous** is checked.

7. Click on the **black** background around Riddick. Let's fill it with a solid color.

8. **Shift–click** on any areas of black background that were not selected to add them to the selection. Don't forget to click between the ropes!

9. If some of the selection cuts into Riddick's body you can do **one** of the following:

    A. Subtract it using the **Lasso** tool ⌁ while holding the **Option** key (Mac) or the **Alt** key (Windows).

    B. Switch into **Quick Mask Mode** ▣:

    • Double–click the **Quick Mask Mode** button ▣ and make sure Color Indicates: **Selected Areas**. Click **OK**.

    • Use the **Brush** tool ✐ to paint **white** over any shaded areas of Riddick's body.

    • When done with the selection, switch back to **Standard Mode** ▣.

10. With the selection complete, select the **Eyedropper** tool ⌇.

11. To sample some of the dark background color near Riddick's head, click once on the image.

12. To fill the selected area with the sampled foreground color, you can either:

    • Go into **Edit > Fill** and for **Contents**, choose **Foreground Color**. Then click **OK**.

    • Or just hit **Option–Delete** (Mac) or **Alt–Delete** (Windows).

13. To deselect, press **Cmd–D** (Mac) or **Ctrl–D** (Windows).

Adding More Blank Area to the Right Side

1. Go to **Image > Canvas Size** and set the following:

    Width: Set the measurement to **Percent**, and enter **200**

    Height: Leave as is

    Canvas extension color: **Foreground**

    Anchor: Click the **left-middle** arrow as shown below.

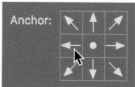

2. Click **OK**.

Making the Ropes Fade Out

1. We want to fade the ropes to the right of Riddick's left leg to black. We'll do this with a gradient, but first we want to create a new layer for it, so go ahead and click the **Create a new layer** button ▣ at the bottom of the Layers panel.

2. Double–click on the new layer's name and type in **rope fade**.

3. Choose the **Gradient** tool ▣ (you may need to click and hold on the **Paint Bucket** tool ▣ to find it).

4. At the left of the **Options** bar, find the gradient preview. As shown below, click the arrow to its right.

5. Double–click the **second** thumbnail on the left in the top row, which is the **Foreground to Transparent** gradient. (If you pause a moment over the thumbnail, the name will appear.)

6. Also in the **Options** bar, choose:

   • **Linear Gradient** ▣

   • Mode: **Normal**

   • Opacity: **100%**

   • **Dither** and **Transparency** should be checked.

7. With the **Gradient** tool ▣, click and drag from the right edge of the ropes to the left edge (stop before you reach Riddick's shorts), along the angle of the ropes.

Creating a Custom Pattern for His Shorts

Now let's make a pattern to place on Riddick's shorts.

1. Go to the **Layers** panel and click on the **Background** layer to select it.

2. Using the **Rectangular Marquee** tool ▣, draw a marquee around both gloves.

3. Copy the gloves (**Cmd–C** (Mac) or **Ctrl–C** (Windows)).

4. Go to **File > New**.

5. In the new dialog under Background Contents, choose **Transparent**, then click **Create**.

6. Paste the selection (**Cmd–V** (Mac) or **Ctrl–V** (Windows)).

7. In the **Tools** panel, click and hold on the **Magic Wand** tool [icon] and then select the **Quick Selection** tool [icon].

8. The Quick Selection tool will work like the Magic Wand but allows you to paint a selection by clicking and dragging. In the **Options** bar at the top of the screen, pick a medium-sized (about **25 px**), hard-edged brush.

9. To select the glove, start in the center of the right glove and click and drag. Keep dragging around until the entire glove is selected.

10. If you've accidentally selected anything additional, hold **Option** (Mac) or **Alt** (Windows) and click and drag on the parts you want to deselect.

11. Click and drag inside the left glove to select it too.

12. In the **Tools** panel, click the **Default Colors** icon [icon] to make sure the Foreground color is pure black and the Background color is pure white.

13. To clean up the selection we'll use Quick Mask Mode. At the bottom of the **Tools** panel, double–click the **Quick Mask Mode** button [icon].

14. In the dialog that appears:

    • Make sure Color Indicates: **Selected Areas**.

    • Under **Color**, make sure the swatch is a bright color like red or green. If not, click on the swatch and choose a bright color that will stand out against the image.

15. Click **OK** to close the Quick Mask Options.

16. Use the **Brush** tool [icon] to paint **black** over any missed areas of the gloves you want selected, and press **X** to switch to **white** and paint over to deselect any areas.

17. When done with the selection, click **Edit in Standard Mode** [icon].

18. Go to **Select > Inverse**.

19. Press **Delete** (Mac) or **Backspace** (Windows).

20. Press **Cmd–D** (Mac) or **Ctrl–D** (Windows) to deselect.

21. Go to **Edit > Free Transform**.

22. The Scale options now appear in the **Options** bar at the top of the screen. In the Scale area, between the Width and Height values, click the **Maintain aspect ratio** button [icon] to keep it from distorting the image.

23. For Width, enter a value of **20%**. Then click the **checkbox** [icon] at the right of the Options bar (or press **Return** (Mac) or **Enter** (Windows)).

24. With the **Rectangular Marquee** tool [icon], draw a box around the gloves that is a little bigger than the gloves.

25. Go to **Edit > Define Pattern**.

26. Name it **yourname-boxing gloves** and click **OK**.

27. We'll leave this file open just in case we need it later, but now switch back to the **Riddick Bowe** file. If you can't see it, go into the **Window** menu and at the bottom, choose **Riddick Bowe**.

Filling the Shorts with a Pattern

Riddick's shorts are a little boring, so let's add that boxing glove pattern.

1. In the **Layers** panel, make sure the **Background** layer is still selected.

2. Click and hold on the **Quick Selection** tool and select the **Magic Wand** tool. Set the Tolerance to **50**.

3. Click somewhere on the light part of Riddick's shorts.

4. **Shift–click** on a few other light areas of the shorts to add them to the selection. Ignore the darker wrinkles for now.

5. In the **Tools** panel, click the **Edit in Quick Mask Mode** button.

6. Choose the **Brush** tool.

7. In the **Options** bar, set the **Opacity** and **Flow** to **100%**.

8. Pick a medium-sized, hard-edged brush.

9. You'll want shading across the entire surface of Riddick's shorts, so use **black** to add shading over the missing wrinkles, sections of the waistband, and any other missing areas. Paint over the words on the trunks, too.

10. If areas outside the shorts (such as the ropes) are selected, type **X** on the keyboard to swap the Foreground and Background colors. Now paint **white** over any shaded areas outside those shorts.

11. In the **Tools** panel, click the **Edit in Standard Mode** button.

12. In the **Layers** panel, click the **New fill or adjustment layer** button and choose **Pattern**.

13. Your boxing gloves pattern should already be selected, so click **OK**. If it wasn't selected, click the pattern thumbnail and choose it.

14. The shorts look very flat right now, but Blending Modes can change the way in which the pattern blends with the shorts. At the top of the **Layers** panel, change the Mode from **Normal** to **Multiply**.

    With the **Multiply** blending mode, this layer can only darken the image behind it, so the dark areas of the shorts on the background layer show through. Feel free to experiment with other blending modes to compare the results.

15. The gloves are still a little bright. At the top of the **Layers** panel, next to the Blend Mode, change the **Opacity** to **60%**.

16. If you decide you'd like to reposition the pattern within the shorts, go to the **Layers** panel and **double–click** the layer's thumbnail 🖼.

    With the **Pattern Fill** dialog box open, click and drag on the main image to move the pattern. Click **OK** when you're done.

17. Congratulations—Riddick would be proud! Save this as a Photoshop document if you wish.

Exercise Overview

A standard print image is CMYK and has a resolution of 300 ppi (pixels per inch). Digital camera images are RGB and often come in as 72 ppi or higher. We will modify an image taken with a digital camera and properly prepare it for print.

1. From the **Photoshop Class** folder, open the file **koala.jpg**.

2. Go to **Image > Mode > CMYK Color**. If you get a message, click **OK**.

3. Go to **Image > Image Size**. Do NOT click OK until we say!

4. Notice that the **Resolution** for this file is **72** but the **Document Size** is **32.444** by **48.667** inches. This means you'd get a large print, but low quality.

5. At the bottom, uncheck **Resample**.

6. For Resolution, type **300**. You'll see that the **Document Size** reduces to **7.787** by **11.68** inches. This means you'd get a smaller print, but high quality.

   That's the largest size this photo can be printed at full quality. It was important to uncheck Resample (which means to add, remove, or recalculate pixels). We don't want to add/remove pixels. Instead, we're shrinking the pixels. At 300 ppi, pixels are too small to be seen. Refer to the sidebar at the end of the exercise for more info.

7. Click **OK**.

8. Go to **File > Save As**.

9. Use the following instructions to save this image as a **PSD** (**Photoshop Document**) or **TIFF**. What's the difference? PSD works great with other Adobe apps. TIFFs are more widely accepted in non-Adobe programs and often have slightly smaller file sizes if LZW compressed. Both maintain full image quality.

Save As PSD

1. Under **Format** (Mac) or **Save as type** (Windows), choose **Photoshop**.

2. Name it **yourname-koala.psd** and click **Save**.

3. If asked to maximize compatibility, leave it checked on and click **OK**.

Save As TIFF

1. Under **Format** (Mac) or **Save as type** (Windows), choose **TIFF**.

2. Name it **yourname-koala.tif** and click **Save**.

3. Set **Image Compression** to **LZW** then click **OK**. LZW is a lossless compression that shrinks file size while maintaining full image quality. It's widely accepted, but may not be compatible with all applications.

---

10. Close the file.

Changing Size & Resolution

Resampling OFF: As shown below, turn off resampling to change the size of pixels, instead of adding or removing them. Small pixels = clean, crisp prints.

15 pixels @ 1"
= 15 ppi

15 pixels @ 0.5"
= 30 ppi

15 pixels @ 0.16"
= 90 ppi

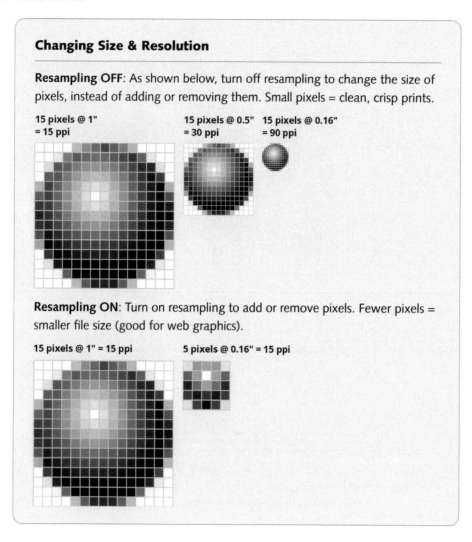

Resampling ON: Turn on resampling to add or remove pixels. Fewer pixels = smaller file size (good for web graphics).

15 pixels @ 1" = 15 ppi

5 pixels @ 0.16" = 15 ppi

Exercise Preview

Exercise Overview

Many times, the same content will be used for both print and web and needs to be converted appropriately. Web images use RGB color and a resolution of 72 ppi, which corresponds to the number of pixels per inch that monitors display. Also, when you're saving images for the web, file size becomes an important issue. Larger files take longer to download!

Resizing an Image for the Web

1. From the **Photoshop Class** folder, open the file **opera house.tif**.

2. Before making this web-ready, it's a good practice to save a copy. Go to **File > Save As**.

3. Next to **Format** (Mac) or **Save as type** (Windows), choose **Photoshop**.

4. Name it **yourname-opera house-web.psd** and click **Save**. If changes are needed further on, you now have a clean original copy you can use to re-save for the web.

5. Go to **Image > Mode > RGB Color**.

6. Go to **Image > Image Size**.

7. Notice that the **Resolution** is 300. We need something less for the web.

8. At the bottom, check on **Resample**.

> **Resampling**
>
> **Resampling** means to **add**, **remove**, or **recalculate** pixels.
>
> When **Resample** is **checked**, the number of pixels actually changes. Either pixels are removed, creating an image with less pixel information, or pixels are added—these "made-up" pixels often result in a less detailed, more blurry image.
>
> When it is **unchecked**, resizing or changing the resolution of the image will not affect the number of pixels in the image—but you can convert a large printing, low-resolution image to a smaller printing, high-resolution version, or vice versa.

9. From the **Resample** menu, choose **Automatic**.

   Behind the scenes, Photoshop will automatically choose **Bicubic Sharper** because we'll be reducing the image's size. This helps maintain a bit more sharpness than **Bicubic**.

10. Next to Resolution, type **72**.

    Notice that the number of pixels have been reduced. We don't need all of them so resampling will throw out/recalculate the reduced number of pixels we need.

11. Make sure **Constrain Aspect Ratio** 🔒 is depressed.

12. Set **Width** to **400** pixels, making sure to set **Pixels** as the units. The height will change automatically to maintain the proportions of the image.

13. Click **OK**.

Setting JPEG Quality in the Save for Web Dialog

1. Go to **File > Export > Save for Web (Legacy)**.

   NOTE: **Save for Web** is now marked as **Legacy** because Adobe won't be updating it to support new features such as artboards. In CC 2015 Adobe introduced brand new exporting methods such as **File > Export > Export As**. These new methods may be suitable in some cases, but they are currently not as developed and lack some options found in **Save for Web**. Adobe is keeping **Save for Web** until the new methods can fully replace it. For what we're doing in this book, we prefer **Save for Web** for its more complete feature set.

2. A new window appears, allowing you to adjust compression settings and preview the final image. Click the **4-Up** tab at the top.

3. You're now looking at the original, uncompressed image in the upper left of the window, and three compressed versions, each using a different setting. Click on the **upper right** image.

4. In the settings on the right, from the menu **below Preset**, choose **JPEG**.

   NOTE: The JPEG format is best for photos. It maintains good quality at a small file size. Be careful, though—the more you compress JPEGs, the more they will degrade and visual distortions will appear.

5. For the **Quality** setting on the right side of the window, type **100**.

   Note that the file size appears under each of the compressed preview images. While this doesn't cause much visual distortion, we can get a much smaller file if we try a lower quality.

6. Click on the **lower left** image. Choose **JPEG** and set the Quality to **0**.

   This is too distorted for most purposes, but the file size is small!

7. Click on the **lower right** image. Choose **JPEG** and set the Quality to **70**.

   This is getting closer. There's only minor distortion. The trade-off between quality and file size reaches a good balance here.

8. Notice that there's a thicker border around the **lower right** image preview area. That indicates it's the selected version. Click **Save** to save a copy of this one.

9. Make sure it's named **yourname-opera-house-web.jpg**.

   NOTE: When naming files for the web, DO NOT use spaces in the filename. Spaces will cause problems with web browsers. Use dashes or underscores instead. Photoshop will automatically replace any spaces with dashes.

10. Navigate to the **Photoshop Class** folder and click **Save** (Format: **Images Only**).

11. You should now be looking at the original Photoshop file. Go to **File > Save**. This will save the JPEG quality settings. So if changes need to be made later, it will remember the Save for Web settings we used for this specific file!

12. Close the file.

Exercise Preview

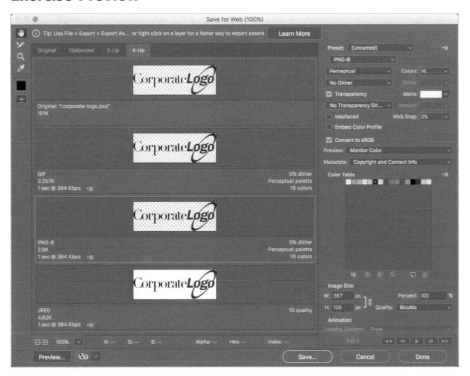

Exercise Overview

Photographs and images with many colors optimize better as JPEGs, but files with few colors (or areas of flat solid color) are ideal for GIF or PNG compression.

Saving as GIF

1. From the **Photoshop Class** folder, open the file **corporate-logo.psd**.

2. Although this image is already in **RGB** mode at **72 ppi**, we should crop out the empty pixels to make the file size smaller. We could use the **Crop** tool and trim it manually, but there's a better way. Go to **Image > Trim** and set the following:

3. Click **OK**, and Photoshop quickly and precisely trims the image for you!

4. Go to **File > Export > Save for Web (Legacy)**.

5. In the settings on the right, from the menu **below Preset**, choose **GIF**.

   The GIF format shrinks file size by reducing the total number of colors in an image. GIFs may have up to 256 colors, but generally you'll need far fewer than that.

6. From the **Colors** setting on the right, choose **16** Colors.

7. From the menu to the left of **Colors**, choose the **Perceptual** color palette.

   Adaptive, **Selective**, and **Perceptual** base their color choices on the actual image. The other options are preset color palettes and therefore are typically not desirable. We chose Perceptual in this case because it was the smallest file size, and visually there was almost no difference between the three options.

8. The **Dither** option uses scattered pixels to represent intermediate colors and often makes gradual blends look smoother. We don't need that in this image, so in the menu immediately below **Perceptual**, choose **No Dither**.

9. From the **Matte** menu, choose whatever color you'd want to use as the background of your imaginary website (in this case, white).

   GIF transparency does not allow for partial transparency. Therefore, any partially transparent pixels must become opaque. The Matte color is used as a background blend color for any pixels that are partially transparent in the original image. Choosing a color similar to your background allows the edges to better blend with the background of the webpage it will be used on.

10. Make sure that the **Transparency** checkbox is checked.

11. Choose the **Zoom** tool 🔍 on the left side of the window.

12. Click on the image to zoom in. The formerly translucent pixels around the edge of the logo have been blended with the **Matte** color to form completely opaque pixels!

Comparing GIF to PNG-8

GIF and PNG-8 compressions work almost exactly the same, but PNG is newer. PNG files are often smaller than GIFs but not always. Since all the settings are the same, we can do a quick test right now to see which is better for this graphic.

1. Take note of the GIF's current file size.

2. In the settings on the right, from the menu **below** the **Preset**, change **GIF** to **PNG-8**.

3. Notice how the PNG is smaller? In our experience, a PNG with the same settings as a GIF is typically 5–25% smaller. For regular text, GIF is sometimes smaller, so you should typically do a test and go with whichever format yields a smaller file size.

4. Click **Save** and save it as **yourname-logo.png** in the **Photoshop Class** folder.

   For more information about color palettes and the GIF, PNG, and JPEG formats, refer to the **Web File Formats** reference at the back of this workbook.

Exercise Preview

Exercise Overview

There are many ways to improve a photograph with Photoshop's powerful color correction tools, some of which are easier to understand than others. This exercise will introduce you to a couple of the more intuitive techniques like Color Balance and Brightness/Contrast.

Intro to Color Correction

1. From the **Photoshop Class** folder, open **couple of koalas variations.tif**.

    This file is a good visual aid to help beginners wrap their heads around color correction. It takes practice to start knowing which colors need to be adjusted in an image.

2. Take a moment and notice which examples look better and which colors need to be added or removed.

3. Close the file when you're done.

Adjusting Color Balance

1. Open **couple of koalas.tif**.

2. Go into **Layer > New Adjustment Layer > Color Balance**.

3. Click **OK**.

   The **Properties** panel will open with the Color Balance settings, as shown in the preview image at the beginning of the exercise. The default values are all zero.

4. You may have noticed in the example image that the More Cyan square looked better. Let's start by adding more cyan. Drag the **Cyan/Red** slider to the left and set it at **–40**.

5. Now it's looking a bit yellow. To remove yellow, we have to add blue. Drag the **Yellow/Blue** slider to the right and set it at **+10**.

   The highlights are still a little warm, so let's cool them off by adding blue.

6. From the menu next to **Tone**, choose **Highlights**.

7. Drag the **Yellow/Blue** slider to **+20**.

Adjusting Brightness/Contrast

1. Let's brighten it up a bit. Go into **Layer > New Adjustment Layer > Brightness/Contrast**. Click **OK** to create a new layer.

2. On the right, in the **Properties** panel, move the **Brightness** slider to the right and set it to **10**.

3. Click the **eye** next to each of your adjustment layers a few times to view the difference. These koalas look much healthier now!

4. Do a **File > Save As** and name it **yourname-koalas.psd**, making sure to set **Format** (Mac) or **Save as type** (Windows) to **Photoshop**.

Color Correction Using Levels

Exercise Preview

BEFORE

AFTER

Exercise Overview

Levels offers more fine-tuned control than Brightness/Contrast and Color Balance. This exercise walks you through using Levels to fix a photo's color and contrast.

Adjusting Levels with White, Black, & Gray Points

1. From the **Photoshop Class** folder, open **Chef.jpg**.

2. At the bottom of the **Layers** panel, click the **Create new fill or adjustment layer** button ⊘ and from the pop-up menu, choose **Levels**.

3. Levels will open in the **Properties** panel on the right. You'll see a Histogram, or graph, showing the distribution of shadows (left), midtones (middle) and highlights (right) in the image.

4. Click the **Set White Point** button 🖋 to the left of the histogram.

5. In the image, click on an area that **should** be white. Try to use the lightest area of the chef's clothing.

   The image will lighten. If it's lightened far too much, simply click elsewhere in the image to set a different white point instead.

6. Click the **Set Black Point** button 🖋 to the left of the histogram.

7. In the image, click on an area that **should** be black. Use the darkest area you can find—perhaps the chef's hair or eyes, or maybe a shadow in the bowl of peppers.

   The image will darken. If it's darkened far too much, simply click elsewhere in the image to set a different black point instead.

8. Click the **Set Gray Point** button ![icon] to the left of the histogram.

9. In the image, click on an area that ought to be a perfectly neutral gray. Try the chef's clothing or the backdrop behind her. Experiment by clicking on different areas until you're happy with the results.

   NOTE: While most images have a true white and a true black, they do NOT always have a true neutral gray. So the Set Gray Point tool isn't used as often as the Set White/Black Point tools.

Advanced Experimentation with Histogram Sliders

You've just practiced a quick technique for using levels. If you are going for precise adjustments, though, you may want to use the sliders below the Histogram.

1. Find the **White Point** slider △ just below the Histogram. Slide it to the **left**.

   You'll find that the image becomes lighter as more and more of the light areas become pure white.

2. Move the slider back to the right and the image darkens again.

3. Find the **Black Point** slider ▲ just below the Histogram. Slide it to the **right**.

   You'll find that the image becomes darker as more and more of the dark areas become pure black.

4. Move the slider back to the left and the image lightens again.

5. Find the **Gray Point** (gamma) slider ▲ just below the Histogram.

   • Slide it to the **right**—the image becomes overall darker.

   • Slide it to the **left**—the image becomes overall lighter.

6. To adjust the color balance, go to the top of the Levels dialog box and change the channel from RGB to **Red**.

7. Move the sliders to the right to darken the image by removing red. Move them to the left to lighten the image by adding red.

   Experiment further if you like; but remember that the black, white, and gray point eyedroppers are an easy way to use Levels to improve contrast and fix color casts.

Color Correction Using Curves

Exercise Preview

BEFORE

AFTER

Exercise Overview

Using Curves to adjust an image may be less intuitive, but it is probably the single most powerful color correction tool Photoshop offers.

Adjusting Curves

1. From the **Photoshop Class** folder, open **shawl.jpg**.

2. At the bottom of the **Layers** panel, click the **Create new fill or adjustment layer** button ⊘ and from the menu, choose **Curves**.

3. In the **Properties** panel on the right, you'll see a "curve" line (that is currently straight) comparing the image's original range of shadows, midtones, and highlights (input) to the corrected range (output). Again, the easy approach here is to use those eyedroppers, but we'll adjust them a bit before we use them.

4. Double–click the **Set White Point** button 🖊 near the left of the panel.

5. Under the H,S,B settings, make the **B** (for brightness) setting **96%**. Click **OK**.

   If you get a message about saving the new target color as a default, click **Yes**.

6. In the image, click on an area that **should** be white (or in this case, nearly white). Try to use the lightest area of the woman's shawl.

   The image will lighten. If it's too light, click elsewhere to set a different white point.

7. Double–click the **Set Black Point** button 🖊 near the left of the panel.

8. Set the brightness (B) to **4%**, then click **OK**.

   If you get a message about saving the new target color as a default, click **Yes**.

9. Click on the darkest point in the image, perhaps in the woman's hair.

   The image will darken. If it's too dark, click elsewhere in the image to set a different black point instead.

10. Click once on the **Set Gray Point** button 🖉 near the left of the panel.

11. In the image, click on an area that ought to be a perfectly neutral gray. Try clicking on different areas until you're happy with the results.

    NOTE: Remember that while most images have a true white and a true black, they do NOT always have a true neutral gray. So the Set Gray Point tool isn't used as often as the Set White/Black Point tools.

Working with Midpoints

Curves can do just about anything that Levels can do, with one added advantage: the ability to manipulate multiple midpoints.

1. In the **Properties** panel, you may see multiple diagonal lines.

2. Click on the **Properties** panel menu ☰ and choose **Curves Display Options**.

3. In the dialog box next to **Show** make sure **Channel Overlays** is **unchecked**.

4. Click **OK**.

5. Only one diagonal line should be left visible. Click on the **upper right** point of the line. This is the **White Point**.

6. Drag the White Point to the **left**; you'll find that the image becomes lighter as more and more of the light areas become pure white (it's like moving the white point in Levels).

7. Drag the White Point **downward**; you'll find that the lightest parts of the image are now a duller gray, rather than a pure white.

8. Move the point back to the upper-right corner to return the image to its previous appearance.

9. Click on the **bottom left** point of the diagonal line. This is the **Black Point**.

10. Drag the Black Point to the **right**; you'll find that the image becomes darker as more and more of the dark areas become pure black (it's like moving the black point in Levels).

11. Drag the Black Point **upward**; you'll find that the darkest parts of the image are now a duller gray, rather than a pure black.

12. Move the point back to the bottom-left corner to return the image to its previous appearance.

13. Click on the **middle** of the diagonal line. There's now a new point on the line. Congratulations—you've just created a midpoint that you can manipulate!

14. Drag the midpoint **downward**—the image becomes **darker** overall.

15. Drag the midpoint **upward**—the image becomes **lighter** overall.

16. Remember, Curves allows multiple midpoints. Click on the diagonal line, somewhere between the Black point and the existing midpoint. There's now a second point on the line!

17. Move this midpoint up or down to watch the dark areas of the image (but not pure black areas) get darker or lighter.

18. Perhaps we don't really need to control a second midpoint for this image after all. Click on your latest midpoint and drag it out of the window. Release the mouse button and that midpoint control is gone.

19. Note that at the top of the Curves dialog box, there is a menu for changing the channel from RGB to Red, Green, or Blue (just as in Levels). This can be useful for correcting color casts, but often you'll be able to do a pretty good job with the eyedroppers alone.

20. Go ahead and experiment with different curve shapes.

Proper Curves

The way that you adjust the curves will be different for each unique image, but there are some general curve shapes that tend to work much better than others. Each of the potentially good examples here would have a very different effect on the image.

Potentially Good: **Usually Bad:**

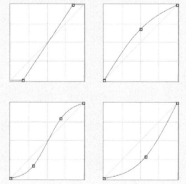
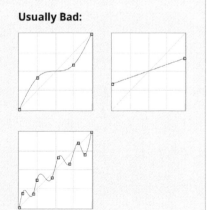

Exercise Preview

BEFORE

AFTER

Exercise Overview

What a horribly washed-out image! We are going to make some color adjustments, but this time we'll use Adjustment Layers to gain more flexibility for future editing.

Adjusting Overall Colors & the Blue Channel

1. From the **Photoshop Class** folder, open the file **na pali coast.tif**.

2. Go to **View > Fit on Screen** (**Cmd–0** (Mac) or **Ctrl–0** (Windows)).

3. At the bottom of the **Layers** panel, click on **Create new fill or adjustment layer** , and from the menu, choose **Curves**.

4. You will see the curves open in the **Properties** panel, as shown below. You may need to resize the window to see all these options.

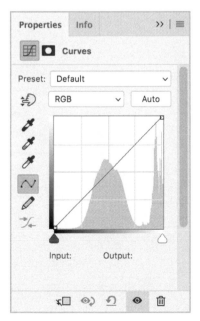

5. Most of the screenshots in this exercise show Photoshop's lightest interface instead of the default medium dark interface. Throughout the book, we may use the light interface when it improves the print quality. (Interface brightness can be changed by going into the **Photoshop CC** menu (Mac) or **Edit** menu (Windows), choosing **Preferences > Interface**, and clicking on the desired **Color Theme**.)

6. Now we are ready to do some color correction. Let's start by properly setting our white and black points, then adjusting the contrast. Look at the histogram and notice in the bottom-left corner that it has no peaks. This means there are no pixels that are black or very dark gray.

7. As shown below, to fix this, hold **Option** (Mac) or **Alt** (Windows) while you drag the **Black** point slider ♠ to the right.

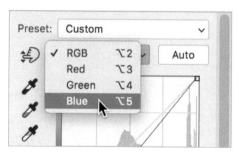

   The image will turn white, but as you get close to the beginning of the histogram's "hill," some small pixels will start to appear in various colors. When you see a few of the colored pixels appear, stop dragging. Those pixels have now been set to black.

8. The photo looks a little cool and bluish. At the top of the **Properties** panel, where it now says **RGB**, choose **Blue** as shown below.

9. Click in the center of the curve and **drag down** a bit to take out some of the blue.

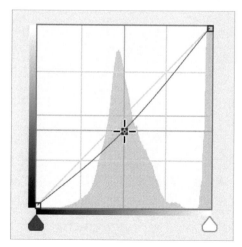

10. In the **Layers** panel, double–click on **Curves 1** and rename it **contrast & color**.

11. The sky is still too bright, but the rest looks good. At the bottom of the **Layers** panel, click on **Create new fill or adjustment layer** and choose **Curves**.

12. Looking at just the sky for reference, make the following adjustment:

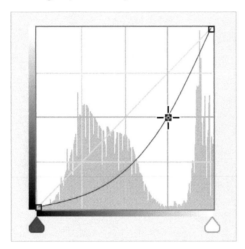

Make sure that the sky looks good, and don't worry about the land. We'll be hiding (masking out) any unwanted areas in a moment.

13. In the **Layers** panel, double–click **Curves 1** and rename it **sky**.

Masking Out Unwanted Adjustments

1. In the **sky** layer, click the **layer mask thumbnail** so it is highlighted, as shown below. You will see that it is highlighted when brackets appear around the empty white box. We are going to edit this layer mask.

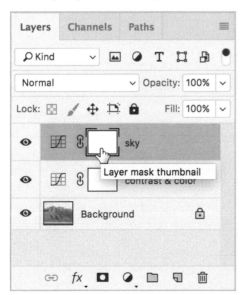

2. Choose the **Gradient** tool ▣.

3. At the left of the **Options** bar, click the arrow ▾ next to the gradient preview to open the gradient panel, and double–click the **third** thumbnail on the left in the top row, which is the **Black, White** gradient.

4. Also in the **Options** bar, choose:

   • **Linear Gradient** ▣

   • Mode: **Normal**

   • Opacity: **100%**

   • **Dither** and **Transparency** should be checked.

5. Starting one third of the way up from the bottom (around the brown dirt), drag **up** to the top of the mountain range.

6. The black on the mask has hidden the darkening effect of this adjustment layer at the bottom, and the mask's white has made it visible at the top. There may be parts we want to darken or lighten. Choose the **Brush** tool ▱.

7. In the **Tools** panel, click the **Default Colors** icon ▣.

8. In the **Options** bar, choose a huge brush (at least **250 px**) with **0% hardness**.

9. Also in the **Options** bar, lower the **Opacity** to **20%**.

10. Painting white with a 20% Opacity on the mask will slowly reveal the darker **sky** curves adjustment. Paint anywhere that looks a little bright to darken it a bit.

11. Likewise, press **X** to swap the Foreground and Background colors so you have **black**. Now paint anywhere that looks too dark to mask that layer and brighten it up.

Organizing Layers into Groups

We want to see what the image looks like without our adjustments to get a sense of what we've done, but before doing that, let's do one more thing to jazz up this photo. We want that Hawaiian foliage to really pop out!

1. At the bottom of the **Layers** panel, click on **Create new fill or adjustment layer** ◕, and from the menu, choose **Hue/Saturation**.

2. In the **Properties** panel, move the **Saturation** slider to the right to somewhere between **10–20**. Experiment with what you think looks best. We want to add color but not make it look fake.

3. We'd like to compare the final image to the original. A nice way to do this (and keep the file organized) is to put the layers into a Layer Group. In the **Layers** panel, make sure the top layer is still selected.

4. Hold **Shift** and click on the **contrast & color** layer. All three adjustment layers should now be selected.

5. Go into **Layer > Group Layers** (**Cmd–G** (Mac) or **Ctrl–G** (Windows)).

6. In the **Layers** panel, you should now see a folder. Double–click the folder's name and change it to **my adjustments**.

7. Click the **arrow** ❯ to the left of the **my adjustments** layer group to expand it and see that your layers are inside.

8. Click the **eye** 👁 beside the **my adjustments** layer group a few times to hide and show all the layers it contains. This lets you see a before and after. Pow!

   When you see the background layer without the effect of the adjustment layers, it's clear that the original layer is unchanged. Adjustment layers allow flexibility of editing, and they preserve the original image!

9. **File > Save As** as **yourname-na pali coast.psd**, setting **Format** (Mac) or **Save as type** (Windows) to **Photoshop** to maintain layer editability.

Exercise Preview

BEFORE

AFTER

Exercise Overview

This image is way too dark—you can't see the sign at all! We will use the Shadows/Highlights adjustment to make the sign legible and the image properly balanced. We'll also learn about Smart Objects.

Creating a Smart Object

When possible, we like to use adjustment layers for color corrections. Oddly, the Shadows/Highlights adjustment we want to use is not an adjustment layer! However, Photoshop offers a different way to apply this adjustment non-destructively using Smart Objects.

1. From the **Photoshop Class** folder, open the file **Hershey trolley stop.tif**.

2. Go to **Layer > Smart Objects > Convert to Smart Object**.

3. In the **Layers** panel, change the name of **Layer 0** to **Hershey**.

The Shadows/Highlights Adjustment

1. There are many dark parts of the image that need to be lightened. Go into **Image > Adjustments > Shadows/Highlights**.

2. Even the default options make the image look better, but we can tweak things more. At the bottom of the window, check on **Show More Options**.

3. Play around with the settings to adjust the image as desired. If you need some advice, here are some settings we think look nice:

Shadows

Amount: **45%**

Tone: **57%**

Radius: **34 px**

Highlights

Amount: **6%**

Tone: **73%**

Radius: **39 px**

Adjustments

Color: **+20**

Midtone: **+5**

4. Click **OK** when done.

5. Let's see how much of a difference we made. In the **Layers** panel, under the **Hershey** layer, you should see the **Shadows/Highlights** adjustment listed.

6. Click the **eye** next to **Shadows/Highlights** a few times to see the before/after.

7. Make sure the **Shadows/Highlights** adjustment is visible before continuing.

Removing the Adjustment Where You Don't Want It

There may be some parts of the image where you don't like the adjustment. We'll use the Smart Filter's mask to hide it. That way we can un-hide it later if we decide we want the adjustment back.

1. As shown below, in the **Layers** panel, click on the **Smart Filters** layer mask. The brackets around it indicates the mask thumbnail is selected.

2. Choose the **Brush** tool .

3. In the **Tools** panel, click the **Default colors** icon .

4. Also in the **Tools** panel, click the **swap colors** icon .

5. The **Foreground** color should now be pure **black** and the **Background** color pure **white**. It's important to remember how layer masks work:

   • Painting with **black = hide**.

   • Painting with **white = reveal**.

   • Painting with a shade of **gray = partially hide**.

   Paint anywhere you want to hide the adjustment, such as the shadow area of the trees on the right of the image.

6. If you hid some of the adjustment and then realized you shouldn't have, you can either go to **Edit > Undo** or paint with **white** to reveal the adjustment again.

7. Nice—that looks so much better! You can close the file, saving if you wish.

Exercise Preview

BEFORE

AFTER

Exercise Overview

The photo shown above is slightly out of focus. While Photoshop can't fix horribly blurry pictures, it can make adjustments to improve photos like this.

The Smart Sharpen Filter

1. From the **Photoshop Class** folder, open **Heather portrait.tif**.

2. Do a **File > Save As** and name the file **yourname-Heather portrait.psd**. Set **Format** (Mac) or **Save as type** (Windows) to **Photoshop**.

3. Go to **View > 100%** to see the most accurate view of the image.

4. Go to **Filter > Sharpen > Smart Sharpen**.

5. Move the window so you can see as much of the photo in the background as possible. When previewing, it's best to look at the actual image rather than the preview box.

6. Enter the following but do NOT click OK yet!

   Amount: **400%**

   Radius: **3 px**

   Reduce Noise: **10%**

   Remove: **Lens Blur** (this often yields a finer, more subtle sharpening)

7. **Check** and **Uncheck Preview** a few times to get an idea of how the sharpening looks. Notice the light/dark halos around some of the elements in the photo, especially the window and the shoulder on the right. Their unnatural look means we're applying too much sharpening.

8. Change Radius to **1 px**.

9. **Check** and **Uncheck Preview** again to see the change. At 1 px, the halos are not so dramatic.

10. Experiment with the Amount and Radius to find the combination that you think looks best. We recommend somewhere around **250% amount** and **1 px radius**. Of course, images that are in focus require a lower amount and radius.

11. When finished, click **OK**, then **File > Save** and close the file.

Sharpening Hi-Res Photos for Print

When dealing with high resolution photos used for print, a slightly higher radius is typically used.

1. Open **do not feed the animals.jpg**.

2. Do a **File > Save As** a **Photoshop document** named **yourname-do not feed the animals.psd**.

3. Go to **View > 100%** to see the most accurate view of the image.

4. Go to **Filter > Sharpen > Smart Sharpen**.

5. Move the window so you can see as much of the photo in the background as possible.

6. Enter the following but do NOT click OK yet!

    Amount: **250%**
    Radius: **1.5 px**
    Reduce Noise: **10%**
    Remove: **Lens Blur**

7. **Check** and **Uncheck Preview** a few times to see how the sharpening looks. The texture really pops out with this amount of sharpening. Since some sharpening can be lost when printing, it's OK to go slightly heavy on the sharpening.

8. When finished, click **OK**, then save and close the file.

Exercise Preview

Exercise Overview

In this exercise, you are going to use text to mask a photo, so the image will only be revealed within the type. Then you'll enhance the type even further by adding some nifty special effects.

Masking a Photo with Type

1. From the **Photoshop Class** folder, open the file **grandCentral.jpg**.

2. To create a solid backdrop for the design, we'll use a fill layer. This is a special kind of layer that is just used to fill an area with a solid color. At the bottom of the **Layers** panel, click the **Create new fill or adjustment layer** button ⬤, and from the menu, choose **Solid Color**.

3. In the **Color Picker** that appears, choose **white**. (The initial color is based on the current foreground color.)

4. Let's change the Background layer into a normal layer so we can work with it. In the **Layers** panel, double–click on the **Background** layer. In the dialog box that appears, change **Layer 0** to the name **photo** and click **OK**.

5. Drag the **photo** layer above the **Color Fill** layer, to put the photo on the top of the layer stacking order.

6. Select the **Horizontal Type** tool ⬛.

7. Click in the image and type the following, as shown (on 2 lines):

   GRAND
   CENTRAL

8. Select all the text (**Select > All**).

9. In the **Character** panel (**Window > Character**), choose a thick font, such as **Impact**. Choose a font size that allows the text to stretch across most of the photo and a leading that looks comfortable for the font size. Remember, if you can't find the value you need, you can either type numbers directly into each field, click in a field and use the Up and Down Arrows on your keyboard, or hover over the icon next to the menu and click and drag with the hand slider 🖑 .

10. Move the type until it's positioned where you like it. If you have problems seeing the type, try changing its fill color in the **Character** panel or **Options** bar. It doesn't matter what color the text is—you won't see this color in a moment.

11. Once the text is positioned, go to the **Layers** panel and drag the type layer underneath the **photo** layer.

12. Hold the **Option** (Mac) or **Alt** (Windows) key and position the cursor on the divider line between the **text** layer and **photo** layer. When the cursor changes to a **Clipping Group** icon (as shown below), then **click**.

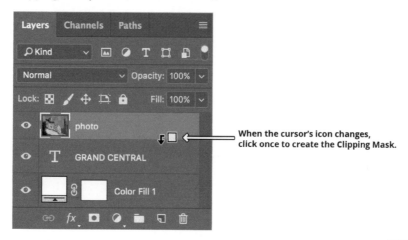

When the cursor's icon changes, click once to create the Clipping Mask.

13. You will see that the type has "masked" the photo. With the **Move** tool ⊕ , move either the **text** or **photo** layer until the layout looks best to you.

Adding Special Effects

1. Let's put a glow around the text. Select the **type** layer and click the **Add a layer style** button 𝑓𝑥 . From the menu, choose **Outer Glow**.

2. In the dialog box that appears, set the following:

   • Change the Blend Mode to **Normal**.

   • Click the white color box (under Noise) to bring up the **color picker**. Choose any color that looks good to you.

   • Adjust the other Outer Glow settings as you like.

3. Click **OK**.

4. Congratulations! If you'd like to experiment further with layer styles, you can create your own special effects to add to this.

5. If you save the file, you should choose the **Photoshop** (.psd) format to preserve editability.

Saving for Use in InDesign or QuarkXPress

We want to ensure that the type in this image prints as well as possible! It's best to print it as resolution-independent vectors, rather than pixels. As vectors, it will output crisp and clean at the full resolution of the output device. That leaves us with only two file formats that support printable vectors: **Photoshop EPS** and **Photoshop PDF**.

If you save as an **EPS**, you'll see a dialog that has an option (checked by default) to **Include Vector Data**, which preserves the vector data in the file, including text and vector paths. The drawback to EPS files is they don't support layers or semi-transparency. Since they don't support layers, you'll need to keep a copy of the layered Photoshop (.psd) file in case you need to make edits.

If you save as a **Photoshop PDF**, however, you get it all: vector printing, layer support, full editability, and semi-transparency. When doing a **File > Save As**, set the **Format** (Mac) or **Save as type** (Windows) to **Photoshop PDF**, click **Save**, and make sure you set these important settings:

1. At the top of the window, set the Adobe PDF Preset to **[Press Quality]**.

2. On the left, click on **Compression** and:

   • Change **Bicubic Downsampling To** to **Do Not Downsample**.

   • Set **Compression** to **None**.

3. On the left, click on **Output** and:

   • Set **Color Conversion** to **No Conversion**.

4. After you save, if it asks if you want to **Preserve Photoshop Editing Capabilities**, just click **Yes**.

TIP: We recommend you save these settings as a preset, so in the future you can choose it from the **Adobe PDF Preset** menu. To do that, on the bottom left of the window, click the **Save Preset** button and name it something like **Photoshop File for Page Layout Program**.

Exercise Preview

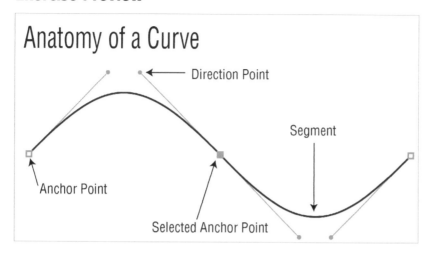

Exercise Overview

This exercise gives you an overview of the Pen tool. You'll draw some basic curves (known as Bézier curves) using the template we have made for you. It's easy once you know how!

1. From the **Photoshop Class** folder, open the file **curves template.psd**.

2. Choose the **Pen** tool .

3. In the **Options** bar, on the left, select **Path** in the dropdown menu. (A path refers to a combination of as many Bézier curves as you want.)

Bézier Curve Drawing Tips

This file is a template for you to trace so you get practice drawing Bézier curves. Here are some tips to keep in mind as you draw:

1. In part A, you will **drag** from the numbered black points to the red circle. This must be done in ONE motion: press down (without releasing) on the black point and hold while dragging to the red circle.

2. If you mess up, just undo it.

3. When done drawing one line, do any **one** of the following to deselect the line before continuing on to draw the next line:

   • Hit the **Escape** (**Esc**) key.

   • Switch to the **Path Selection** tool and click off the line to deselect it.

   • Hold **Cmd** (Mac) or **Ctrl** (Windows) (a shortcut to get the Direct Selection tool) and click off the line to deselect it.

4. Each section removes some of the "training wheels" so you get a chance to get better at judging how far to drag, and in what direction.

5. If you finish and want to try tracing the lines again, just go to **File > Revert** and your work is erased so you can start tracing them fresh again.

   NOTE: For more tips on drawing Bézier curves, please refer to the **Drawing Paths** reference at the back of the book.

Exercise Preview

Exercise Overview

We need to remove the background from this horseshoe so we can add it to a print design that has been created in InDesign. (While you can do most of the steps if you don't have InDesign, you will not be able to do the entire exercise.) The smooth, crisp edges of the horseshoe are perfect for a clipping path.

NOTE: If you are working on these exercises out of order, we highly recommend completing **Exercise 5C** before starting this one.

Creating a Path Around an Object with the Pen Tool

1. From the **Photoshop Class** folder, open the image **horseshoe.tif**.

2. Go to **View > Fit on Screen** (**Cmd–0** (Mac) or **Ctrl–0** (Windows)) so the horseshoe is nice and big, filling most of the screen. This will make it easier to draw.

3. Choose the **Pen** tool ![pen tool icon].

4. In the **Options** bar, make sure that **Path** is selected.

5. Starting at the top of the right side, click and drag out a handle upwards and right.

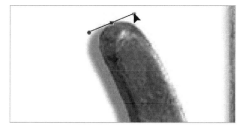

6. Below on the right, click and drag the next point to follow the contour of the curve.

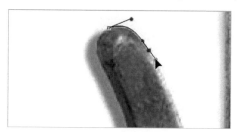

7. Continue this process around the entire horseshoe, except the last point. As you proceed, remember the following tips:

   • If you make a mistake, just undo by pressing **Cmd–Z** (Mac) or **Ctrl–Z** (Windows).

   • Try to place points slightly inside the edge of the horseshoe to avoid including any of the white background.

   • Longer handles make larger curves, smaller handles make smaller curves.

   • Perfection is not necessary as we'll clean it up in a few steps.

8. When you reach the final point, position the cursor over the first point—it will turn into 🖋₀ . Click and drag up and right toward the anchor handle to finish the shape.

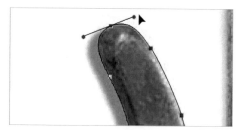

9. Choose the **Direct Selection** tool �. To find it, you may need to click and hold on the **Path Selection** tool ▸.

10. Click once on the path to select it.

11. Clean up the path by:

   • Selecting individual points to move them.

   • Selecting a point, then moving anchor handles to reshape curves.

Turning the Work Path into a Clipping Path

The path you just created is called a Work Path. Only one Work Path can exist at a time, so it must be saved before creating a new path. Once saved, it can be turned into a clipping path.

1. Open the **Paths** panel by going to **Window > Paths**.

2. Double–click on **Work Path**.

3. Name it **horseshoe** and click **OK**.

4. In the **Paths panel menu** ▤, choose **Clipping Path**.

5. From the **Path** menu, select **horseshoe**, leave the **flatness** value blank, and click **OK**.

> **The Flatness Value**
>
> By leaving the flatness value blank, the path will be printed at the full resolution of the output device. Very complicated paths may yield PostScript errors, however. If you get an error while printing, input a flatness value to decrease the complexity and try again (the higher the flatness value, the more it simplifies the path).

Saving & Importing the Image into InDesign

To save this file, we need to choose a file format appropriate for InDesign. When using clipping paths in InDesign, many file types work (like PSD, TIFF, or EPS). If you're unsure, we recommend you go with a Photoshop file (PSD).

1. Go to **File > Save As**.

2. Navigate into the **Kissimmee Brochure** folder.

3. Under **Format** (Mac) or **Save as type** (Windows), choose **Photoshop** and name the image **yourname-horseshoe.psd**.

4. Launch **InDesign** (if you have more than one version, launch **CC 2018**).

5. Go to **File > Open**. From the **Kissimmee Brochure** folder, open the InDesign file **Brochure-add horseshoe.indd**.

6. Using the **Selection** tool ▶, select the rectangular picture box near the bottom left. It's an empty blue box with an X through it. It's bigger than the **Did You Know** text box.

7. Go to **File > Place**.

8. Go to the **Kissimmee Brochure** folder and double–click **yourname-horseshoe.psd**.

9. Go to **View > Display Performance > High Quality Display**.

10. Zoom in and enjoy your nice, crisp vector edges.

11. We no longer need this file, so close the InDesign file and do NOT save changes. You're done!

Exercise Preview

Exercise Overview

We will use a Layer Mask to remove the background from around a picture of a hat. Layer Masks offer the most editing flexibility and they are non-destructive. This exercise also involves importing into InDesign. You can do most of the steps if you don't have InDesign, but you will not be able to finish the exercise.

Selecting the Hat

1. From the **Photoshop Class** folder, open the image **hat.tif**.

   Notice how part of the hat's brim is not in focus, and some areas of the background are a similar color to the hat. With a combination of selection tools and layer masks, even a challenging silhouetting task like this is a piece of cake!

2. Choose the **Magnetic Lasso** tool .

3. In the **Options** bar, make sure it has the following settings:

Feather:	**0 px**
Width:	**10 px**
Contrast:	**10%**
Frequency:	**57**

4. Click **once** along the brim to start the lasso selection. (Do not click and hold.)

5. Move the cursor along the edges of the hat, and the lasso will lay down points along the path as the cursor moves. Keep in mind the following tips:

   • When you reach a corner or tricky place, click to manually place a point.

   • Press **Delete** (Mac) or **Backspace** (Windows) to back up and delete points that have been placed incorrectly.

6. When you reach the end, place the cursor over the first point, so it changes to a 🔗 and click to finish the selection.

7. In the **Options** bar, click the **Select and Mask** button.

8. In the **Properties** panel on the right, click on the thumbnail next to **View** and double-click **On Black**.

9. Set **Opacity** to **100%**.

10. In the **Edge Detection** section, make sure **Radius** is set to **0 px**.

11. In the **Global Refinements** section, set the following:

    Smooth: **10**
    Feather: **0.5 px**
    Contrast: **0%**
    Shift Edge: Around **–40%**, but experiment with what looks best for you.

12. In the **Output Settings** section, make sure **Output To** is set to **Layer Mask**.

13. Click **OK**.

14. In the **Layers** panel, notice the Background layer has been changed into a regular layer with a new name (**Layer 0**) and a layer mask has been added.

    NOTE: Background layers cannot be transparent or have layer masks, so the **Select and Mask** feature converted it into a normal layer for us!

15. In the **Layers** panel, double-click the **Layer 0** layer and name it **hat**.

16. At the bottom of the **Layers** panel, click the **Create new fill or adjustment layer** button ⬛, and from the menu, choose **Solid Color**.

17. Choose **black** and click **OK**.

18. In the **Layers** panel, click and drag the **Color Fill 1** layer below the **hat** layer.

Cleaning Up the Edges

There may be spots showing through from the old background, and the brim edge should be softer. Let's start by fixing the top part of the hat. Later we'll fix the brim.

1. In the **Layers** panel, double-click the **Color Fill 1** layer's thumbnail ⬛.

2. Set the following RGB values:

   R: **0**
   G: **70**
   B: **100**

3. Click **OK**.

4. In the **Layers** panel, click the hat layer mask .

5. Select the **Brush** tool .

6. In the **Options** bar, choose a **small-sized**, **fairly hard** brush. We recommend about **8 px diameter** and **90% hardness**. This size will let you get into the corners nicely.

   Make sure **Opacity** and **Flow** are set to **100%**.

7. Press **D** to set the default white and black foreground and background colors.

8. Press the **X** key to switch the foreground/background colors so the foreground color is **black**.

9. Paint over areas where you see the original light background color around the hat (zoom in as needed). This will remove it, kind of like you are erasing it.

10. As needed, reduce the brush size to get into corners, etc.

11. If you removed any parts of the hat and want to reveal them, remember:

    • Paint **white** over any parts you want to reveal (like the hat).

    • Paint **black** over any parts you want to hide (like the background).

    • Press the **X** key to switch the foreground and background colors.

Finishing Up

The front and back of the brim are blurry in the photo, but the edge of our mask makes them look crisp.

1. Select the **Blur** tool .

2. In the **Options** bar, choose a **medium-sized soft brush** (about **40 px, 0% hardness**).

3. Click and drag to blur the edges of the brim in the front and back.

4. In the **Layers** panel, select the **Color Fill 1** layer.

5. Drag it to the **Trash** button to delete it. Now you should be left with a transparent checkerboard background.

Importing the Image into InDesign

To save this file, we need to choose a file format appropriate for InDesign.

1. Go to **File > Save As**.

2. Navigate into the **Kissimmee Brochure** folder (inside the **Photoshop Class** folder).

3. Set **Format** (Mac) or **Save as type** (Windows) to **Photoshop** and name the image **yourname-hat.psd**. Click **Save**.

   NOTE: TIFF can also work, but you must check on **Save Transparency**.

4. Launch **InDesign** (if you have more than one version, launch **CC 2018**).

5. From the **Kissimmee Brochure** folder, open the InDesign file **Brochure-add hat.indd**.

6. Choose the **Selection** tool ⬚.

7. On the bottom left, click on the empty rectangular picture box.

8. Go to **File > Place**.

9. Choose **yourname-hat.psd** and click **Open**.

10. Go to **View > Display Performance > High Quality Display**.

11. Zoom in and examine the blurry, semi-transparent parts. Very nice.

    Enjoy your work—you're done! Because we no longer need this file, close the InDesign file and do NOT save changes.

Exercise Preview

Exercise Overview

While the original Miata photo we will edit in this exercise is pretty good by itself, it would be even better with some sense of motion. We'll use various filters to simulate motion and make the car "pop!"

Blurring the Background

1. From the **Photoshop Class** folder, open the file **miata.tif**.

2. We'd like to give this image a sense of speed and motion, so we'll use a couple of filters to alter the image. Go to **Select > Load Selection**.

3. In the dialog box that appears, choose the channel **car silhouette**, and check on **Invert**. Click **OK**.

4. Go to **Layer > New > Layer Via Copy**. Now, in addition to the original background layer, there is a layer containing everything except the car.

5. Go to **Filter > Blur > Motion Blur**.

6. Set the following:

    Angle: **–15°**
    Distance: **40 Pixels**

7. Click **OK**.

8. In the **Layers** panel, double–click on the name of **Layer 1** and rename it **blurry bg**.

Spinning the Wheels

1. Click back on the **Background** layer to highlight it.

2. Choose **Select > Load Selection**.

3. In the dialog box that appears, choose the channel **front wheel**. Make sure **New Selection** is selected. Click **OK**.

4. Go to **Layer > New > Layer Via Copy**.

5. Name the new layer **front wheel**.

6. Hold **Cmd** (Mac) or **Ctrl** (Windows) and click on the **front wheel** layer thumbnail in the Layers panel. This selects all opaque pixels in the layer.

7. Go to **Filter > Blur Gallery > Spin Blur**.

8. In the **Options** bar, make sure **Preview** is checked on.

9. A blur area with overlay controls and a preview of the blur will appear on the photo. Drag the rotation point (center of the blur area) to the center of the hubcap:

NOTE: We don't need to do this for the current image, but you should know that the rotation point can also be moved off-center. To move it off-center hold **Opt** (Mac) or **Alt** (Windows) when dragging.

10. Over the next few steps we'll adjust the shape of the blur area. Before we start, here's how we want the final shape to look like:

11. First let's make the whole blur area smaller. Hover over the thin white line (not any of the dots) so the cursor looks like this resize handle ⬉.

12. Drag the thin white line in towards the center of the blur area to make it slightly larger than the car's wheel.

13. We need to better match the shape and angle of the wheel, so let's make the blur area into an oval shape that is tilted slightly to the left. Hover over the small outer dot on the right of the blur area so the cursor looks like this resize handle ↰.

14. Drag this dot in towards the center to make the blur area slightly narrow.

15. Drag the top small outer dot away from the center to make the blur area a bit taller.

16. Tilt the blur area slightly to the left by dragging any of the small white outer dots counter-clockwise.

    NOTE: You can also adjust how much of the selection gets blurred using the feather handles (large white dots). The further away from the blur area's edge they are, the less of the selection will get blurred. We want the whole hubcap to be blurred so there's no need to adjust the feather handles.

17. To adjust the amount of the blur, hover anywhere inside the blur area to reveal a **black/white circular slider** that surrounds the center point. As shown below, drag the slider until you're satisfied with that amount of blur.

    NOTE: You can also adjust the **Blur Angle** in the **Blur Tools** panel on the right.

18. In the **Options** bar, on the right, click **OK** to apply the blur. Now we're cruisin'!

19. Click back on the **Background** layer to highlight it.

20. Choose **Select > Load Selection** and:

    • Choose the channel **back wheel**.

    • Make sure **New Selection** is selected, then click **OK**.

21. Go to **Layer > New > Layer Via Copy**.

22. Name the new layer **back wheel**.

23. Hold **Cmd** (Mac) or **Ctrl** (Windows) and click on the **back wheel** layer thumbnail in the **Layers** panel.

24. Once again, go to **Filter > Blur Gallery > Spin Blur**.

25. Adjust the blur area as needed, then change the Blur Angle to your liking.

26. When you're done, click **OK** in the **Options** bar.

That's it! You've taken a static image and used filters to give it an illusion of speed and motion. What a rush!

Exercise Preview

THE FINAL GOAL

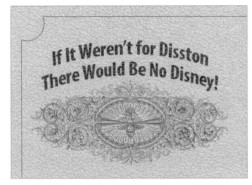

PART I - HEADER, DECORATION, & BORDER

Exercise Overview

In the next few exercises, we are going to build a brochure from elements found in a number of files. In this first part, we'll make the background, border, and header text. We will also add some decoration to enhance the old-timey look.

Making a Textured Background

1. From the **Photoshop Class** folder, go into the **Kissimmee Brochure** folder and open the file **Kissimmee brochure.psd**.

2. Go to **File > Save As**, go into the **Kissimmee Brochure** folder, and name it: **yourname-Kissimmee brochure.psd**.

3. If the guide we added for you in the middle of the document is hidden, go to **View > Show > Guides**.

4. At the bottom of the **Layers** panel, click the **Create new fill or adjustment layer** button, and from the menu, choose **Solid Color**.

5. Enter the following CMYK values:

   C: **12** M: **31** Y: **62** K: **0**

   Click **OK**.

6. Double–click directly on the name **Color Fill 1** and rename it **bg color**.

7. Open the file **leather texture.tif**.

8. Select all by pressing **Cmd–A** (Mac) or **Ctrl–A** (Windows).

9. Copy by pressing **Cmd–C** (Mac) or **Ctrl–C** (Windows).

10. Close the file and return to **yourname-Kissimmee brochure.psd**.

11. Paste by pressing **Cmd–V** (Mac) or **Ctrl–V** (Windows).

12. Double–click directly on the name **Layer 1** and rename it **leather**.

13. With the **leather** layer selected, at the top left of the **Layers** panel, change the blending mode from **Normal** to **Overlay**. Overlay lightens where the image is lighter and darkens where the image is darker.

14. The leather texture is a little too pronounced. In the **Layers** panel, lower the **Opacity** to around **70%**.

Making a Selection 20 Pixels from the Edge

1. **Select All** by pressing **Cmd–A** (Mac) or **Ctrl–A** (Windows).

2. Go to **Select > Modify > Contract**.

3. Check on **Apply effect at canvas bounds**.

4. Enter **20** and click **OK**. Now we have a selection exactly 20 pixels from the edge of the document which we will use to build our border.

Creating a Border

1. Choose the **Elliptical Marquee** tool.

2. In the Options bar, from the **Style** menu, choose **Fixed Size** and enter **60 px** for **Width** and **Height**.

3. Let's subtract some circle shapes from the four corners of the selection. Hold **Option** (Mac) or **Alt** (Windows) and **click and hold down** while you **drag** the circle into the upper-left corner, then release when you see two intersecting pink Smart guides (as shown below).

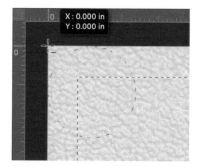

4. Continue this process for the remaining three corners. Hold **Option** (Mac) or **Alt** (Windows) and click and drag the circle into the corner, then release.

5. In the Options bar, change the **Style** from **Fixed Size** back to **Normal**.

6. In the **Layers** panel, click the **Create new fill or adjustment layer** button , and from the menu, choose **Solid Color**.

7. Choose **white** and click **OK**.

8. Double–click directly on the name **Color Fill 1** and rename it **page border**.

9. Click the **Add a layer style** button *fx* and from the menu, choose **Stroke**.

10. Set the following options:

    • Size: **1 px**

    • Position: **Outside**

    • Click the color swatch and enter the following CMYK values:
      C: **31** M: **61** Y: **100** K: **18**

11. Click **OK**, then **OK** again to close the Layer Style dialog.

12. Near the top right of the **Layers** panel, reduce the **Fill** to **0%**. This should remove the white but leave the border.

13. Depending on your zoom level, the border might disappear in certain areas. Choose **View > 100%** to see how things really look.

Adding the Header

1. Scroll to the top-left corner of the document.

2. Press **D** to set **black** as the foreground color.

3. Choose the **Horizontal Type** tool ⊞.

4. In the **Options** bar, make the font **Myriad Pro**, **Bold Condensed**, **25 pt**, and click the **Center text** button ☰.

5. Near the top, centered in the left "column" of the document, click once to place the cursor. Type the following two lines of text:

   If It Weren't for Disston
   There Would Be No Disney!

6. Select all the lines of text and go to **Window > Character**.

7. In the **Character** panel, set the **Leading** ⊞ to **26 pt**.

8. In the **Options** bar, click the **Create warped text** button ⊞.

9. In the dialog that opens, from the **Style** menu, choose **Arc** and set the following:

    Bend: **+21%**

    Horizontal Distortion: **0%**

    Vertical Distortion: **–2%** (that's negative 2)

    Click **OK**.

10. If it's there, click the **checkbox** ✓ at the right of the **Options** bar to finish.

11. Use the **Move** tool ✛ to position the text so it is centered at the top of the left column.

12. To capture the texture of the leather for the text we'll use a piece of the leather as our mask. At the bottom of the **Layers** panel, click the **Add layer mask** button ▣.

13. In the **Layers** panel, select the **leather** layer.

14. Choose the **Rectangular Marquee tool** ⬚.

15. Drag a selection box that covers all the text plus some extra.

16. Copy by pressing **Cmd–C** (Mac) or **Ctrl–C** (Windows).

17. Hold **Option** (Mac) or **Alt** (Windows) and click the warped text's white **layer mask** to enter that mask. If done correctly, the document will be completely white.

18. Paste by pressing **Cmd–V** (Mac) or **Ctrl–V** (Windows).

19. In the **Layers** panel, click the warped text thumbnail to exit the mask.

20. To get rid of the selection, press **Cmd–D** (Mac) or **Ctrl–D** (Windows).

21. Zoom in so you can see how the mask looks.

Bringing in Some Decoration

1. Open the file **ornamentation.tif**.

2. Select all by pressing **Cmd–A** (Mac) or **Ctrl–A** (Windows).

3. Copy by pressing **Cmd–C** (Mac) or **Ctrl–C** (Windows).

4. Close the file and return to **yourname-Kissimmee brochure.psd**.

5. Paste by pressing **Cmd–V** (Mac) or **Ctrl–V** (Windows).

6. Double–click directly on the name **Layer 1** and rename it **banner ornament**.

7. With the **banner ornament** layer selected, change the blending mode from **Normal** to **Multiply**.

   NOTE: The Multiply blend mode always darkens. White disappears, while other colors darken whatever is underneath.

8. Choose the **Move** tool ⊕ .

9. Position the ornamentation so it is centered under the text. (Release the mouse when you see a vertical Smart Guide.)

10. Go to **File > Save** and leave the file open. We will continue with it in the next exercise.

    Tighten up those bootstraps, partner; the next part could get pretty wild!

_____

Exercise Preview

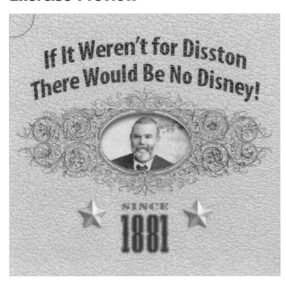

Exercise Overview

In this exercise, we will bring in a photo and fit it into the oval in the center of our decorative banner. We don't know exactly what size we'll want in the end, so placing in a Smart Object is going to be the most flexible option.

Welcome, Mr. Disston!

1. You should still have the **yourname-Kissimmee brochure.psd** file open. If you closed it, re-open it now. If you haven't done the previous exercise:

   • From the **Photoshop Class** folder, go into the **Kissimmee Brochure** folder and open **Kissimmee Part 1 done.psd**.

   • Save it as **yourname-Kissimmee brochure.psd**.

2. In the **Layers** panel, make sure the **banner ornament** layer is selected.

3. Go to **File > Place Embedded**.

   NOTE: **Place Embedded** adds a copy of the placed file into the current Photoshop document as a smart object. If you share the Photoshop file with someone else, they will not need the original file to edit the smart object. **Place Linked** retains a link to the original file on your computer. When changes are made to that linked file on your computer, Photoshop will prompt you to update the smart object. If you share the Photoshop file with someone else, you would also need to give them the linked file for them to be able to edit the linked smart object.

4. From the **Kissimmee Brochure** folder, choose **portrait.psd** and click **Place**.

5. Press **Return** (Mac) or **Enter** (Windows) to accept the size.

6. Click the **eye** 👁 beside the **portrait** layer to hide that layer.

7. Choose the **Elliptical Marquee** tool ⭕.

8. In the **Options** bar, from the **Style** menu, make sure **Normal** is chosen.

9. Place the cursor in the center of the decorative oval.

10. As shown by the arrow below, hold **Option** (Mac) or **Alt** (Windows) and click and drag out an oval selection that fits inside the oval in the file (as indicated by the white dashed line).

11. In the **Layers** panel, click where the eye was beside the **portrait** layer to show it.

12. At the bottom of the **Layers** panel, click the **Add layer mask** button ▣.

13. Click the **link** icon 🔗 between the layer thumbnail and the mask thumbnail to unlink them.

14. Click the portrait layer's **thumbnail** 🖼 to select the image, instead of the mask, which is currently selected.

15. Choose the **Move** tool ✛.

16. Click and drag to move the photo over the oval mask, so you can see his face.

17. Go to **Edit > Free Transform**.

18. Position the cursor over the corner resize handles to get the resize cursor ↖↘.

19. Hold **Shift–Option** (Mac) or **Shift–Alt** (Windows) and drag to resize the photo so you can see his head and shoulders.

20. Move the cursor a little further away from the corner to get the rotation cursor ↰.

21. Click and drag to rotate the photo so that Mr. Disston is straight up and down.

22. When finished, press **Return** (Mac) or **Enter** (Windows) to accept the changes.

23. Click between the layer thumbnail and the mask thumbnail, where the **link** icon 🔗 was before, to link them again.

24. In the **Layers** panel, click the **Add a layer style** button *fx* and from the menu, choose **Inner Shadow**.

25. Make the following changes:

    Opacity: **70%**
    Angle: **90°**
    Size: **6 px**

    Click **OK**.

Editing the Smart Object

1. The portrait is too light. It needs to be darkened. Notice the icon in the **portrait** layer thumbnail. That icon means that the portrait is a Smart Object. Double–click the layer thumbnail to open the Smart Object.

2. A message may appear stating that after making changes in the Smart Object, you should save the file to update changes. Click **OK**.

3. The Smart Object opens in a new window with its own set of layers and adjustments. Notice that the name of this document is **portrait.psd**.

4. In the **Layers** panel, expand the **photo restoration** layer group, and then the **contrast & color** layer group, if they aren't already expanded.

5. Double–click the curve thumbnail in the **contrast** layer (it's in the **contrast & color** group). Now we can edit the curve.

6. In the **Properties** panel, pull the **middle-right** point down to the midline.

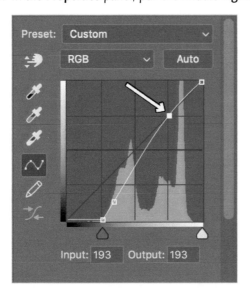

7. Go to **Window > Arrange > 2-up Vertical**. Now you can see both documents open. Take note that the oval portrait in the brochure has not changed.

8. Make sure the **portrait.psd** file is still highlighted and go to **File > Save**. Notice that the portrait in the brochure becomes darker, reflecting the changes you just saved to the smart object.

9. Close the **portrait.psd** file to return to **yourname-Kissimmee brochure.psd**.

Since 1881

1. Open the file **Since 1881.psd**.

2. If you get a message about updating the text layers before they can be used for vector based output, click **Update**.

3. In the **Layers** panel, **Shift–click** the **1881** layer to select both the type layers.

4. Go to **Layer > Group Layers**.

5. In the **Layers** panel, double–click **Group 1** and rename it **Since 1881**.

6. To copy the two text layers into your Kissimmee brochure, do the following:

   • With the Since 1881 group still selected, do an **Edit > Copy**. If Copy is grayed out, refer to the sidebar below.

   • Switch back to **yourname-Kissimmee brochure.psd** using the tab at the top.

   • Go to **Edit > Paste**.

> **In Photoshop CC 2017 & Older**
>
> 1. Make sure both files are open (the file that contains the layer you want to copy and the file you want to put it in).
>
> 2. In the **Layers** panel, **Ctrl–click** (Mac) or **Right–click** (Windows) on the name of the layer you want to move/copy and choose **Duplicate Layers** from the menu that appears.
>
> 3. Set the Destination **Document** to the file you want to move the layer into. (Next to **As**, change the layer name if desired.) When done, click **OK**.

7. Close the **Since 1881.psd** file and don't bother saving changes.

8. Back in the **yourname-Kissimmee brochure.psd** file, make sure the **Move** tool is selected.

9. Use the Smart Guides to help you position the **Since 1881** layer group below the banner ornament.

10. In the **Layers** panel, click the **arrow** next to the **Since 1881** group to view the contents of that group.

11. Select the **1881** layer.

12. Click the **Add a layer style** button fx and from the menu, choose **Stroke**.

13. Set the following options:

    • Size: **2 px**

    • Position: **Outside**

    • Click the color swatch and enter the following CMYK values:
      C: **12** M: **57** Y: **95** K: **5**

14. Click **OK** and **OK** again.

15. In the **Layers** panel, click the **arrow** ∨ next to the **Since 1881** group to hide the contents of that group.

Thank My Lucky Stars

1. Click and hold on the **Rectangle** tool ▦ and choose the **Custom Shape** tool ▨.

2. In the **Options** bar, on the left make sure **Shape** is selected.

3. Photoshop has a built-in star shape, but we must load it first. In the **Options** bar, on the right, click the **Shape** menu.

4. Click the **panel menu** ⚙ and choose **All**.

5. Click **OK** to replace the current shapes with All shapes.

6. Located about halfway down the list is a **5 Point Star** shape ★. Find this shape and double–click on it to choose it.

7. Hold **Shift** and drag out a star to the left of the word **SINCE** as shown below.

8. In the **Layers** panel, double–click **Shape 1** and rename it **star**.

9. Double–click the star's thumbnail and set the following CMYK values:
   C: **4** M: **19** Y: **69** K: **0**

10. Click **OK**.

11. Choose the **Move** tool ✛.

12. Position the star so it looks nice on the left side of **Since 1881**.

13. Click the **Add a layer style** button _fx_ and from the menu, choose **Bevel & Emboss**.

14. Set the following, but DON'T click OK yet:

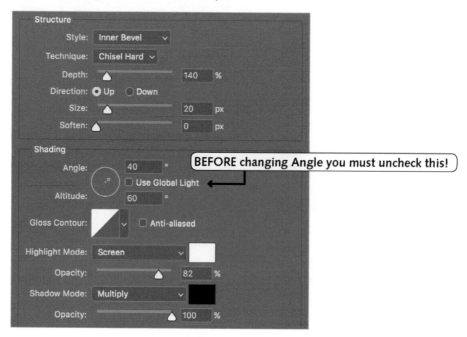

15. On the left side of the window, click on the words **Drop Shadow** so it's checked on and selected. Click directly on the words. Do not just check the checkbox, or else you won't see its options on the right.

16. Set the following:

    Use Global Light: **Uncheck** this first
    Angle: **60°**
    Distance: **1 px**
    Spread: **2%**
    Size: **3 px**

17. Click **OK**.

18. Hold **Shift–Option** (Mac) or **Shift–Alt** (Windows) and drag a copy of the star to the right side of the word **SINCE**.

19. In the **Layers** panel, **Shift–click** on the other star layer.

20. Press **Cmd–G** (Mac) or **Ctrl–G** (Windows) to group the layers.

21. In the **Layers** panel, double–click **Group 1** and rename it **stars**.

22. Go to **File > Save** and leave the file open. We'll continue with it in the next exercise. This rodeo's almost done. There's just one round left, so hang in there, kiddo!

Exercise Preview

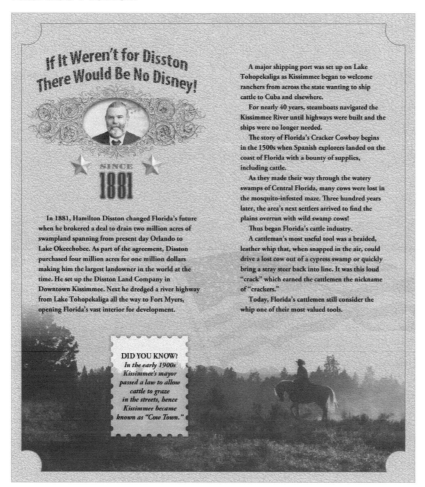

Exercise Overview

In this exercise, you'll add the main text and put finishing touches on the brochure.

Adding the Main Text

1. You should still have the **yourname-Kissimmee brochure.psd** file open. If you closed it, re-open it now. If you haven't done the previous exercises:

   • From the **Photoshop Class** folder, go into the **Kissimmee Brochure** folder and open **Kissimmee Part 2 done.psd**.

   • Save it as **yourname-Kissimmee brochure.psd**.

2. In the **Layers** panel, make sure the **stars** layer group is selected.

3. From the **Kissimmee Brochure** folder, open the file **main paragraphs of text.psd**.

4. If you see a dialog about updating text layers, click **Update**.

5. In the **Layers** panel, select both the text layers (using **Shift–click**).

6. Press **Cmd–G** (Mac) or **Ctrl–G** (Windows) to group the layers.

7. In the **Layers** panel, double–click **Group 1** and rename it **main text**.

8. To copy the layer group into your Kissimmee brochure so they maintain their original positions, do the following:

   • With the main text group still selected, do an **Edit > Copy**. If Copy is grayed out, refer to the sidebar below.

   • Switch back to **yourname-Kissimmee brochure.psd** using the tab at the top.

   • Do NOT paste using the keystroke! To paste the layers exactly where they were in the previous file, go to **Edit > Paste Special > Paste in Place**.

In Photoshop CC 2017 & Older

1. Make sure both files are open (the file that contains the layer you want to copy and the file you want to put it in).

2. In the **Layers** panel, **Ctrl–click** (Mac) or **Right–click** (Windows) on the name of the layer you want to move/copy and choose **Duplicate Layers** from the menu that appears.

3. Set the Destination **Document** to the file you want to move the layer into. (Next to **As**, change the layer name if desired.) When done, click **OK**.

---

9. Close the **main paragraphs of text.psd** file and don't bother saving changes.

10. Back in the **yourname-Kissimmee brochure.psd** file, make sure the **Move** tool ⊹ is selected.

11. The banner ornament, title, date, etc. may need to be re-positioned to look good above the new text. In the **Layers** panel, select the **If It Weren't for Disston There Would Be No Disney!** type layer. It's near the middle of the list.

12. Hold **Shift** and click on the **stars** layer group. (This should select all layers except bg color, leather, page border, and main text.)

13. Press **Cmd–G** (Mac) or **Ctrl–G** (Windows) to group the layers.

14. In the **Layers** panel, double–click **Group 1** and rename it **title and banner**.

15. Move the **title and banner** layer group to a better position in the brochure.

Adding a Cowboy

1. In the **Layers** panel, select the **main text** layer group.

2. From the **Kissimmee Brochure** folder, open the file **cowboy.tif**.

3. Select all by pressing **Cmd–A** (Mac) or **Ctrl–A** (Windows).

4. Copy by pressing **Cmd–C** (Mac) or **Ctrl–C** (Windows).

5. Close the file and return to **yourname-Kissimmee brochure.psd**.

6. Paste by pressing **Cmd–V** (Mac) or **Ctrl–V** (Windows).

7. Double–click directly on the name **Layer 1** and rename it **cowboy**.

8. If the rulers are not already showing, go into the **View** menu and select **Rulers**. If they aren't in inches, **Ctrl–click** (Mac) or **Right–click** (Windows) in the ruler and choose **Inches** from the menu.

9. Hold **Shift** and drag the cowboy layer down until the top is approximately at **5.5 inches**.

10. At the top left of the **Layers** panel, change the Blending mode from **Normal** to **Multiply**.

11. This layer needs to have the same mask as the **page border**. To copy it, hold **Option** (Mac) or **Alt** (Windows) and drag the **page border** layer mask up to the **cowboy** layer as shown below:

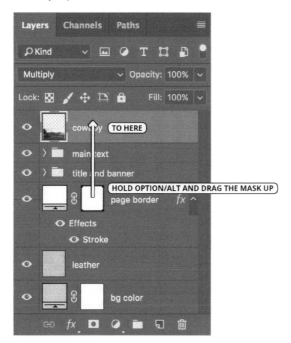

12. In the **Layers** panel, lower the **Opacity** to around **70%**.

13. Let's make the top of the cowboy image blend more smoothly into the background. Choose the **Gradient** tool 🔲.

14. At the left of the **Options** bar, click the arrow ⌄ to the right of the gradient preview and double–click the **second** thumbnail on the left in the top row, which is the **Foreground to Transparent** gradient.

15. In the **Layers** panel, make sure the layer mask is selected.

16. Make sure the foreground color is set to **black**.

17. Position the cursor at the top of the cowboy photo, hold **Shift** and drag down about an inch to **6.5 inches** as shown on the rulers.

18. Click on the **cowboy** layer thumbnail to exit the mask.

Adding a Flag

1. Go to **File > Place Embedded**.

2. From the **Kissimmee Brochure** folder, choose **flag silo.tif** and click **Place**.

3. Position the cursor near a corner of the image, so that it changes into the rotation handles ↰.

4. Rotate to around **–25°** (that's minus 25). The **Options** bar will tell you the angle △. Press **Return** (Mac) or **Enter** (Windows) when finished.

5. At the top left of the **Layers** panel, change the Blending mode from **Normal** to **Multiply**.

6. In the **Layers** panel, lower the **Opacity** to around **7%**.

7. Choose the **Move** tool ✛.

8. Position the flag so it is "flying" above the cowboy, behind some of the right column of text. The right edge of the flag should extend off the page.

Adding a Stamp & Some Text

1. Scroll to the bottom of the image. Make sure you can see the area from the text to the bottom.

2. Choose the **Custom Shape** tool 🎨.

3. In the **Options** bar, on the left, make sure **Shape** is selected.

4. On the right in the Options bar, click on the **Shape** menu.

5. Scroll about halfway and locate the **Stamp 1** shape ☐ and double–click it. (If you can't find it, it's a few rows above the 5 point star and to the right of a paperclip.)

6. Press **X** to switch to a **white** foreground color.

7. Hold **Shift** and **click and drag** out a stamp shape that fills the area below the left column of text.

8. In the **Layers** panel, double–click **Shape 1** and rename it **stamp**.

9. Near the top right of the **Layers** panel, reduce the **Fill** (opacity) to **70%**.

10. Click the **Add a layer style** button *fx* and from the menu, choose **Drop Shadow**.

11. Set the following:

    Distance: **0 px**

    Spread: **0%**

    Size: **7 px**

12. Click **OK**.

13. Choose the **Horizontal Type** tool **T**.

14. Press **D** to get the default black foreground color.

15. Zoom in on the stamp so it's nice and large on the screen.

16. We want to put some text over the stamp. To prevent ourselves from adding text along the stamp path or making a similar mistake:

    • Hold **Shift** as you start dragging a text box inside of the stamp.

    • After you've started the drag, **let go of Shift** so you can make a rectangle.

17. In the Options bar, make the font **Adobe Garamond Pro**, **Bold**, **10 pt**, and click the **Center text** button.

18. Open the **Character** panel (**Window > Character**) and set the **Leading** to **Auto** if it is not already (you'll have to choose it from the menu).

19. Open the **Paragraph** panel (**Window > Paragraph**) and set **Indent first line** to **0** if it isn't already.

20. Type: **DID YOU KNOW?**

21. Press **Return** (Mac) or **Enter** (Windows) to start a new paragraph.

22. In the Options bar, change the font to **Adobe Garamond Pro**, and **Bold Italic**.

23. Type the following line of text:

    In the early 1900s Kissimmee's mayor passed a law to allow cattle to graze in the streets, hence Kissimmee became known as "Cow Town."

24. Notice that the text wraps to fit inside the box? Slick. While holding **Option** (Mac) or **Alt** (Windows), grab one of the corner resize handles and resize the text box so the text wraps as shown below. (If it won't wrap quite right, place the text cursor between "graze" and "in" and hit **Shift–Return** (Mac) or **Shift–Enter** (Windows) to make a new line if necessary.)

> **DID YOU KNOW?**
> *In the early 1900s*
> *Kissimmee's mayor*
> *passed a law to allow*
> *cattle to graze*
> *in the streets, hence*
> *Kissimmee became*
> *known as "Cow Town."*

25. In the **Layers** panel, select the **stamp** layer.

26. Press **Cmd–T** (Mac) or **Ctrl–T** (Windows) to start a free transform.

27. Hold **Shift–Option** (Mac) or **Shift–Alt** (Windows) and drag a corner resize handle to size the stamp so it looks good around the text.

28. Drag inside the stamp to move it or use the **Arrow** keys to carefully nudge it into position.

29. When done press **Return** (Mac) or **Enter** (Windows) to finish.

30. In the **Layers** panel, select both the **stamp** and **"Did you know"** type layer (using **Shift–click**).

31. Press **Cmd–G** (Mac) or **Ctrl–G** (Windows) to group the layers.

32. In the **Layers** panel, double–click **Group 1** and rename it **stamp**.

33. If needed, use the **Move** tool to position the stamp group nicely below the text.

34. Yee-Haw! **Save** the file and you are done.

Optional Experimentation (If You Finish Early)

Try experimenting with the following and see if you can improve the look:

• Add a drop shadow to the **page border** layer.

• Slightly increase the **page border** layer's Fill opacity.

• Change the Fill Color of the **bg color** to modify the color of the leather.

Exercise Preview

BEFORE (NOT MATCHED)

BACKGROUND TO MATCH

AFTER (MATCHED)

Exercise Overview

When you're using photos of similar subjects together in a layout, it's important to have consistency of color between the two images. Photoshop offers an easy way to fix this problem.

Selecting the Areas That Need Color Matching

1. From the **Photoshop Class** folder, open the files **Background-girl.tif** and **Background-guy.tif**.

2. Go to **Window > Arrange > 2-up Vertical** to show the **Background-guy** window next to the **Background-girl** window.

   You're going to make the background around the girl the same color as the background around the guy. First, you'll need to select everything but the people and the TV.

3. Choose the **Quick Selection** tool . If you can't find it, click and hold on the **Magic Wand** tool and then select it.

4. In the **Options** bar at the top of the screen, pick a **medium-sized** (about **9 px**), **hard-edged** brush.

5. Start in the center of the gray background of **Background-guy.tif** and click and drag. Keep clicking and dragging around until the entire background is selected.

6. If you've accidentally selected anything additional, hold **Option** (Mac) or **Alt** (Windows) and click and drag on the parts you want to deselect. Don't worry too much about the chain holding the TV. Some of it will be selected with the background, but that's OK.

7. In the **Options** bar, click **Select and Mask**.

8. Click on the thumbnail next to **View** and double–click on **Black & White**.

9. Set the following:

   Smooth: **10**
   Feather: **2 px**

10. Click **OK**.

11. Switch to **Background-girl.tif** and repeat the process to select the gray background around the woman. Her legs and shoes will probably get selected. When/if that happens, hold **Option** (Mac) or **Alt** (Windows) and click and drag on the parts you want to deselect before you run **Select and Mask**.

Matching Color

1. Go to **Image > Adjustments > Match Color**.

2. At the top of the dialog, make sure **Ignore Selection when Applying Adjustment** is **unchecked**. At the bottom, set the following:

   • For Source, choose **Background-guy.tif**.

   • Make sure **Use Selection in Source to Calculate Colors** is checked.

   • Make sure **Use Selection in Target to Calculate Adjustment** is checked.

3. In the preview, you'll see that the woman's background is now very close in color to the man's. If you feel it's not quite perfect, you can adjust the three sliders:

   • The **Luminance** slider lets you make the woman's background lighter or darker.

   • The **Color Intensity** slider lets you adjust saturation, making the background duller or more vivid.

   • The **Fade** slider allows the original, unadjusted background to show through, giving you a result partway between the original and the fully corrected version.

4. When you're done, click **OK**. Save **Background-girl.tif** if you like. (The image of the guy does not need to be saved since you didn't make changes there.)

   NOTE: The Match Color adjustment is only available in RGB Color mode, not CMYK.

Exercise Preview

BEFORE

AFTER

Exercise Overview

In this exercise, you will take a line art image and prepare it for print. In order to effectively scan detailed line art, one technique is to scan in grayscale. The higher the resolution, the better. If you can scan at 800 ppi, you will probably be OK up to 1200 dpi output. If you scan at higher resolution (such as 1200 ppi) that's better.

1. From the **Photoshop Class** folder, open the image **Alice.tif**.

   NOTE: This image was scanned as grayscale at 600 ppi.

2. Go to **View > 100%**. This will give you the most accurate screen rendition of the image.

Making Adjustments in the Grayscale Color Mode

1. The **Unsharp Mask** filter sharpens images. It increases contrast between adjacent pixels, so it will enhance the art. Go into **Filter > Sharpen > Unsharp Mask** and put in these values:

   Amount: **500%**

   Radius: **1 px**

   Threshold: **5**

2. Click **OK**.

3. Reapply the filter by hitting **Ctrl–Cmd–F** (Mac) or **Ctrl–Alt–F** (Windows). If you like it, leave it. If you think you lost too much ink, undo it.

4. Now go into **Image > Adjustments > Threshold**.

5. Move the slider back and forth until you are satisfied with the preview image. You should find a setting of **128** works well here.

6. Click **OK**.

7. The last step is to convert this image from grayscale to line art. Since all of the pixels are either black or white, we will change to Bitmap color mode to save hard drive space. Go into **Image > Mode > Bitmap**.

8. Leave the Output field at **600**, but under **Method**, make sure **Use** is set to **50% Threshold**. This assures that all black pixels will stay black, and all white pixels will stay white. Click **OK**.

The Despeckle Filter

1. Look at the image. You'll see that the line work is good, but there is a lot of dirt.

   You can clean this manually with the **Eraser** tool ![eraser icon], or you can try using **Filter > Noise > Despeckle** to remove the specks automatically. However, you cannot apply filters in **Bitmap Mode**, and if you use Despeckle, you may lose some detail in your line work. Each drawing reacts differently to Despeckle, so be careful in practice. However, Despeckle works quite well here, so let's try it.

2. First, we must switch out of **Bitmap Mode**. Revert the file to the original by going to **File > Revert**.

3. Before doing anything, just apply the Despeckle Filter. You'll find it under **Filter > Noise > Despeckle**. There is no value setting here, because it is built-in. So just apply it and enjoy. You may not see any difference, but later on, you will.

4. Once you have applied the filter, go back and redo the **Making Adjustments in the Grayscale Color Mode** section. You'll see there is much less dirt. It will now be easier to clean up with the **Eraser** tool ![eraser icon].

   This may not look as nice as the original grayscale image on-screen, but you'll avoid the use of halftone dots in the printing process, giving the image sharp, defined edges. You can use the same process on any other piece of line art!

Exercise Preview

Depending on the print quality of this workbook, you may not be able to see the moiré pattern in this scan. This can also be true for your personal printer. It's best to trust the view on-screen at 100%.

Exercise Overview

When you scan a printed photograph, you often get a moiré pattern due to the presence of a halftone screen. This halftone screen is necessary to print any image on most media. However, there are several options available for avoiding the moiré pattern.

The first option is to use a "descreening" option that comes with your scanner software. This is useful, however, only if your scanning software has such a feature, and even then, the results may be unrewarding. Therefore, other tactics may be needed.

The following method seems to work well for many images. First, the image is scanned at an unusual pixel-per-inch number—say, 718, instead of 300. Then the **Median** filter should be applied to the image. The Median filter can be found in the **Filter** menu, under **Noise**. When you apply this filter, use a radius of 2 pixels. What it does is blend adjacent pixels in the image, equalizing them. This rids the image of some of the variation inherent in the halftone screen. The image will appear to melt together slightly after you apply the filter.

After applying the filter, reduce the image size to the resolution (ppi) you desire—say, 300 ppi for print. The resampling and discarding of aberrant pixels further enhances the smoothness of the image.

Now that you are at the right size, apply the Unsharp Mask filter. A suggested setting is 50% under Amount, a 3-pixel radius, and a 5-pixel threshold. Try this and adjust the settings to your taste.

NOTE: We scanned the file you'll use in this exercise at 359 ppi and we will downsize it to 150 ppi. This is fine for some newspapers but for other print work, you should use the previously stated 718 ppi scanning resolution and 300 ppi should be the final resolution.

To see how this method works on a real scanned image, try this:

1. From the **Photoshop Class** folder, open **Nat Cole.tif**.

2. Go to **View > 100%**. He's been scanned at 359 ppi, and as you can see, a strong dot pattern is evident.

3. First, go to **Filter > Noise > Median**.

4. Make the radius **2** pixels and click **OK**.

5. Next, go to **Image > Image Size** and reduce the image to **150 Pixels/Inch** (ppi).

6. Click **OK**.

7. Finally, go to **Filter > Sharpen** and apply the **Unsharp Mask** filter. Try these settings:

   Amount: **50%**

   Radius: **3 px**

   Threshold: **5**

8. Click **OK**.

9. Save the file as **yourname-Nat Cole.tif**.

10. Open the original and compare them side-by-side by choosing **Window > Arrange > 2-up Vertical**. Make sure they are both zoomed to **100%**. The final image should have a much more natural texture than the original.

Exercise Preview

Exercise Overview

Making a collage in Photoshop involves blending several photos together. You'll remove backgrounds, soften edges, etc. Although you could do this using the Eraser tool or by selecting parts and deleting them, these approaches will delete areas permanently ("destructive" editing). Permanent edits are bad if you want to be able to change your mind later, as we often do! So instead, we'll use masking to hide the pixels instead of deleting them. That way, we can later reveal them if we want.

Importing Images into Your Collage

1. From the **Photoshop Class** folder, open **devinder collage1-started.psd**.

2. Make sure the **Layers** panel (**Window > Layers**) is open.

3. Notice that we've already added one image on top of the main background. We have another image to bring in, so open **devinder on skates.psd**.

4. Select all by pressing **Cmd–A** (Mac) or **Ctrl–A** (Windows).

5. Copy by pressing **Cmd–C** (Mac) or **Ctrl–C** (Windows).

6. Close the file and return to **devinder collage1-started.psd**.

7. Paste by pressing **Cmd–V** (Mac) or **Ctrl–V** (Windows).

8. Back in the **devinder collage**, make sure the **Move** tool 🔛 is selected.

9. In the **Layers** panel, double–click on the name **Layer 1** and rename it **devinder on skates**. (Naming layers in collages is important because you often have many layers, which can get confusing without proper names.)

10. Move the **devinder on skates** layer to the **top-left** corner of the image, releasing the mouse when you see the two intersecting Smart Guides.

11. The image of Devinder in the sand is not in the right place. In the **Layers** panel, select the **devinder in sand** layer.

12. Move it towards the bottom left, but not all the way to the corner.

Turning a Selection into a Layer Mask

1. The image of Devinder in the sand would look nice in an oval frame, so choose the **Elliptical Marquee** tool ⬭.

2. Draw an oval selection around Devinder, making sure no part of the oval falls outside the sand. While drawing the oval, if you find the placement is wrong:

   • Hold the **Spacebar** down and move the oval to the correct place.

   • Then release the **Spacebar** and continue sizing the oval.

3. Once the oval selection is made, you can move it as long as you are in the **Elliptical Marquee** tool ⬭.

4. In the **Layers** panel, make sure you still have the **devinder in sand** layer highlighted.

5. At the bottom of the **Layers** panel, click the **Add layer mask** button 🔲.

   Now you should only see the sand image inside your oval. The rest of the image is still there, but it's hidden by the mask.

Finishing the Oval Image

1. Use the **Move** tool 🔛 to position the oval image so it looks good.

2. Poor Devinder—he's looking away from the image. It looks like he doesn't want to play! Let's make him look more included by facing him inward. Make sure you are still on the **devinder in sand** layer.

3. Go to **Edit > Transform > Flip Horizontal**. That's better!

4. Now that you see how the image looks when it's in the oval, you might want to move it around within the oval to improve the composition.

   As shown below, in the **Layers** panel, click the **link** icon 🔗 between the layer thumbnail and the mask thumbnail.

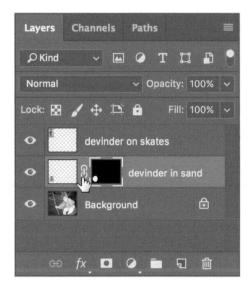

5. Click on the **layer thumbnail** (not the black and white mask thumbnail on the right).

6. Using the **Move** tool ⊕, drag Devinder around. The oval should remain in place while the image of Devinder in the sand moves.

7. Let's add a stroke around the oval to make it stand out more. In the **Layers** panel, make sure the layer is selected and at the bottom of the panel, click the **Add a layer style** button *fx*. From the menu, choose **Stroke**.

8. Set the following options:

   • Set the Size to **3**.

   • Next to Color: Click the color swatch and choose a nice light blue that matches Devinder's blue jacket in the swing picture. (Mouse over the jacket to sample an exact color.)

9. Click **OK** and **OK** again to close the Layer Style dialog.

Creating & Editing a Layer Mask with Gradients & Brushes

1. Let's work on the image of Devinder on his skates. It should be all the way against the top-left corner. If it isn't, move it there now.

2. The right and bottom edges would look better if they softly blended into the background image, so make sure the **devinder on skates** layer is highlighted.

3. At the bottom of the **Layers** panel, click the **Add layer mask** button ⬚. Nothing will change in the image, but in the **Layers** panel there will now be a white mask thumbnail to the right of the layer thumbnail.

4. Choose the **Gradient** tool ⬚ and in the **Options** bar:

   • Click the **Linear Gradient** button ⬚.

   • Set the Opacity to **100%**.

5. At the left of the **Options** bar, click the arrow ⌄ next to the gradient preview.

6. In the top row of the panel that opens, double–click the third thumbnail from the left, which is the **Black, White** gradient. (If you pause a moment over the thumbnail, the name will appear.)

7. As shown below, drag from **right** to **left** over the area where the chain should be. Drag at an angle that is perpendicular to the chain and release.

8. The edge should now fade softly into the chain. If the angle is wrong, just try it again (you don't even have to undo it first!). Just keep trying until you get the fade and angle right.

9. Now for the bottom edge. If we did the gradient fade again for this edge, things might look too straight, boring, and crisp. Let's make the bottom a bit more organic using the brush. Select the **Brush** tool ⬚ and in the **Options** bar, choose an appropriately sized **soft** brush (not a hard-edged brush!).

10. Make the foreground color **black**.

11. Paint around the bottom of the image and watch it fade into the background. Try reducing the Opacity of the Brush (in the Options bar) so you can make the fade nice and smooth, instead of abrupt.

   NOTE: If you remove too much of Devinder, change the **foreground** color to **white** and paint that part back in. Remember the following mask painting tips:

   • By painting with **black** on the mask, you are **hiding** the pixels in that layer.

   • If you paint with **white**, you make them **visible** again.

   • Any shade of **gray partially shows/hides** the layer.

12. That's it—a completed collage! For more practice, continue to the next exercise.

Layer Masking Tips

• When creating a layer mask, select the parts of a layer you want to see. Then click the **Add layer mask** button ▣ in the **Layers** panel: the selected area remains visible, while everything else is hidden by the mask.

• **Shift–click** a mask thumbnail to disable it without throwing it away.

• **Option–click** (Mac) or **Alt–click** (Windows) on a mask thumbnail to view only the mask, not the image.

• **Option–Shift–click** (Mac) or **Alt–Shift–click** (Windows) on a mask thumbnail to view it as a shaded color overlay, much like a Quick Mask.

• Remove a mask by dragging the mask thumbnail to the trash. Photoshop will ask if you want to **Apply mask to layer before removing**. If you click **Apply**, Photoshop will **delete** the areas of the layer that had been hidden by the mask. In most cases, you'll simply want to choose **Delete**, to throw away the mask without affecting the image layer.

Exercise Preview

Exercise Overview

You'll make a collage that looks similar to the one shown above.

More Practice: Making Another Collage

1. If you want another crack at applying layer masks to a collage, from the **Photoshop Class** folder, open **devinder collage2-started.psd**.

   In this starter file, we already have a bunch of images put together. To make your finished collage, here are the things you'll need to do:

2. Blend the various **Duet** layers (the four pictures of Devinder at the top) so they look more seamless (right now they have a harsh line between them). Do this by **adding masks** to the **Duet** layers and then use gradients and/or painting with brushes to hide/show what you want.

   To review the masking rules, when you are painting on a mask:

   • Painting with **black hides** the pixels in that layer.

   • Painting with **white reveals** (shows/unhides) the pixels in that layer.

   • Painting with **gray partially hides/shows** the pixels in that layer.

3. **File > Place Embedded** two more images: **devinder not smiling.psd** and **devinder frog fountain.psd**.

4. Softly blend the edges of these two images into the rest of the image by **adding a mask** and then painting with a **soft** brush of **black** or **white**.

   As you work, be careful of what layer you are on, and whether you are editing the layer or the layer's mask. If you are unsure of which layer is which, try hiding and showing the layer to see which it is.

   If you want to see how we created the finished collage, open **devinder collage2-done.psd** for reference.

Exercise Preview

BEFORE

AFTER

Exercise Overview

Due to varying lighting conditions, you can see this photo has a bad overexposure problem. In order to fix the problem, we will use the image data already provided, merely duplicating it to create an acceptable final image. The idea is that we will double or triple the darkness of the pixels in the overexposed part of the image.

Using Multiply & Layer Masks to Correct Overexposure

1. From the **Photoshop Class** folder, open the file **multiply.psd**.

2. In the **Layers** panel, you will see that this document only has one layer called Background. Duplicate that layer by dragging it onto the **New layer** button ![icon] at the bottom of the panel.

3. Select the new layer, **Background copy**. At the top left of the **Layers** panel, change the **Blending Mode** from **Normal** to **Multiply**. This multiplies the color values of the pixels overlapping each other, so that everything becomes darker.

   Unfortunately, this new layer has made some areas at the bottom of this photo too dark. We'll use a layer mask to hide the parts of the Background copy that make the image too dark.

4. Choose **Layer > Layer Mask > Reveal All**.

5. Choose the **Gradient** tool ![icon].

6. In the **Options** bar, click the **Linear Gradient** button ![icon] and set Opacity to **100%**.

7. Also in the **Options** bar, click the arrow ![icon] next to the gradient preview. Choose the **third** thumbnail from the left in the top row, (the **Black, White** gradient). If you pause a moment over the thumbnail, the name will appear.

8. You're going to add black on the layer mask to hide or "mask" some of the duplicate pixels, so that those areas will not get darker. The **Gradient** tool ▣ is a good choice here because we want a subtle, gradual blend from the light (showing) areas to the dark (hiding) areas of the mask.

   With the **Gradient** tool ▣, drag from the bottom of the image to about halfway up. You'll see the area lighten up, giving the image a more even exposure.

9. After doing it once, you will see whether you did it too much or too little. You can always draw the gradient again if you're not happy. You may have to change the direction, too, dragging from the lower left toward the upper right, in order to get the image to work right. Keep playing with it until you are happy with the result.

More Overexposure? Just Rinse & Repeat!

1. You may notice that there is still a bit too much overexposure at the top of the image. Well, there's no reason you can't make a third copy! Drag the **original Background** layer onto the **New layer** button ▣ again. The new layer will be in the middle of the three.

2. Set the **Blending Mode** to **Multiply**.

3. Then add a layer mask, but this time, HIDE ALL: **Layer > Layer Mask > Hide All**.

4. You'll notice the image is back to what it was before the third copy. That's because all of the doubling effect is hidden by the layer mask. But this time, we are going to use a soft brush to remove parts of the layer mask, and selectively darken the image by letting the new pixels show through. This is somewhat complicated, but once you understand, it is a powerful technique.

5. With **Background copy 2** selected, choose the **Brush** tool ▨.

6. In the **Options** bar, set the Opacity to **25%**. Choose a **soft, 65 pixel** brush.

7. In the **Tools** panel, hit the **Default Colors** icon ▣.

8. In the **Layers** panel, make sure the black **Mask thumbnail** is selected. (It will have brackets around it.)

9. Go to the image and paint white over the areas that you want darkened. Wherever you click or drag, the image will darken. You can always **Undo** if you make a mistake. You mostly want to concentrate on the white strip going across the top, but you may want to touch up other areas of the image as well.

10. Just to get an idea of what you have just done, click on the **eye** ◉ next to the bottom **Background** layer. You will see what you "added" to the image. You can show and hide each layer individually to see what each layer accomplished.

Check Out
OUR OTHER WORKBOOKS!

Web Development
Level 1 and 2

JavaScript & jQuery

GreenSock Animation

Mobile & Responsive
Web Design

WordPress.org

PHP & MySQL

Photoshop for Web & UI

Photoshop Animated GIFs

Sketch

HTML Email

Responsive HTML Email

Ruby on Rails

PowerPoint

Adobe InDesign

Adobe Illustrator

Adobe Photoshop

Photoshop Advanced

Adobe Lightroom

Adobe After Effects

Adobe CC: Intro to InDesign,
Photoshop, & Illustrator

NOBLEDESKTOP.COM/BOOKS

Understanding Color

Color Terminology Defined

Grayscale
A mode in which images are displayed in up to 256 different shades of gray.

HSB
Hue, Saturation, Brightness. Hue is the color tint, Saturation is the amount of color as opposed to gray, and Brightness is the level of lightness, usually measured on a percentage scale, with 0% being black, 100% white.

RGB
Red, Green, Blue. The primary colors of light. They are called additive colors because when added together, they create white—all light is reflected back to the eye. Used with film, lighting, and all video monitors. Monitors emit light through red, green, and blue phosphors to create up to millions of colors.

CMYK
Cyan, Magenta, Yellow, Black. This model is used for most printing. They are called subtractive colors because when light hits them and is reflected, a portion of the light is absorbed. In theory, pure cyan, magenta, and yellow mixed together at 100% will make black, but because of impurities in ink, they combine to make a muddy brown. So it is necessary to also print a premixed black.

Color Gamuts
A color system's gamut is its range of colors. A large color gamut would be the visible spectrum in nature. The RGB model covers a smaller gamut, and therefore computer screens cannot reproduce all colors seen by the human eye. The CMYK gamut is even smaller. It cannot recreate all colors in the RGB gamut. That is one reason a monitor (which is RGB) displays things differently than a print, which is CMYK. Be careful when converting between these as you will lose some color information, although switching from RGB to CMYK is the biggest loss.

Bits
Bit resolution, or pixel depth, determines the amount of color information. 1-bit depth gives you only black or white pixels. 8-bit grayscale gives you up to 256 shades of gray. 8-bit color gives you up to 256 shades of color. 24-bit color gives you up to 16 million colors.

General Strategy for Color Correction

1. Set highlight and shadow points in the image (if needed).

2. Make adjustments to middle tones.

3. Correct for overall color imbalance.

4. Make selective color corrections.

5. Apply sharpening.

_____

Print File Formats Quick Reference

Photoshop (.psd)

PSD stands for Photoshop Document

- Supports all Photoshop features such as: layers, editable type, saved selections, alpha channels, paths, effects, etc.

- Can be semi-transparent (InDesign supports this transparency).

- Type prints as pixels, not vector, at the resolution of the file.

- Supports Duotone when importing into InDesign.

TIFF (.tif)

TIFF stands for Tagged Image File Format

- Optional support for layers.

- Optional support for semi-transparency (InDesign supports this transparency).

- Type prints as pixels, not vector, at the resolution of the file.

- File size is generally smaller than EPS files.

- LZW Compression reduces file size without losing quality.

- Can be colorized in InDesign (with a Pantone color, for example).

EPS (.eps)

EPS stands for Encapsulated PostScript

- Type and vector artwork will print as vectors (prints at full resolution of printing device) instead of pixels.

- Does NOT support layers (it is a flat image).

- File size is generally larger when compared to flat TIFFs or PSDs.

- EPS does NOT support semi-transparency, but does support clipping paths.

- Supports Duotone (works in InDesign).

PDF (.pdf)

PDF stands for Portable Document Format

- Supports all Photoshop features: layers, editable type, saved selections, paths, etc.

Print File Formats Quick Reference

- Supports "printable" vector type (prints at full resolution of printing device).

- In the Save As options, be sure to turn off downsampling, compression, and color conversions.

DCS (.dcs)

DCS stands for Desktop Color Separation

- Rare format; used for spot color work.

- DCS 1.0 creates separate files for each color channel/composite (not recommended).

- DCS 2.0 creates one file; retains spot color channels (recommended).

Web File Formats Quick Reference

Not all of the following file formats or features are available in **Save for Web**. Some can only be exported using **File > Generate > Image Assets** or **File > Export > Export As**. If you plan on designing and optimizing lots of web graphics, you can learn how to use **Generate Image Assets** and **Export As** in our Photoshop for Web Design & UI class or workbook.

JPEG (.jpg)

Good For: Photos and graphics with gradations

Colors: Millions (24-bit)

Transparency: No

Animation: No

Compression: Lossy (loses quality)

JPEG stands for Joint Photographic Experts Group.

PNG-24 & PNG-32 (.png)

Good For: Graphics that require partial transparency

Colors: Millions (24-bit)

Transparency: Yes, including partial transparency. In **Save for Web** PNG-24 has a checkbox for transparency. In **Generate Image Assets** PNG-24 does not have transparency but PNG-32 does.

Animation: No

Compression: Lossless (does not lose quality)

PNG stands for Portable Network Graphic.

PNG-8 (.png)

Good For: Graphics with areas of flat color. Like GIF, but often smaller file size.

Colors: 256 or less (8-bit)

Transparency: Yes, including partial transparency. **Save for Web** does not support partial transparency, but **Generate Image Assets** and **Export As** do.

Animation: No

Compression: Lossless (does not lose quality)

Web File Formats Quick Reference

GIF (.gif)

Good For: Graphics with areas of flat color

Colors: 256 or less (8-bit)

Transparency: Yes, but no partial transparency

Animation: Yes

Compression: Typically Lossless (does not lose quality), although **Save for Web** does have a Lossy option for further compression.

GIF stands for Graphic Interchange Format.

SVG (.svg)

Good For: Vector graphics, such as icons

Colors: Millions (24-bit)

Transparency: Yes, including partial transparency

Animation: Yes (but not from Photoshop)

Compression: Not applicable

SVG stands for Scalable Vector Graphics.

NOTE: Photoshop can create SVG files via **Generate Image Assets** or **Export As**, but the layer must be a native Photoshop vector (not a vector smart object). SVG is not an option in **Save for Web**. If you have a vector file that you want to save as SVG, the easiest way is to use Adobe Illustrator (do a **File > Export > Export As**).

Drawing Paths in Photoshop

Follow These General Rules When Creating Paths

- When setting an anchor point, place it between bumps.

- Always drag in the direction of the next curve.

- When tracing, stick to the outside of curves. Never cross the curve.

- Drag direction points about one-third of the way around a curve.

- As a rule, concentrate on good placement of the new direction point, not the result curve of the previous curve. You can always go back and fix the previous curve.

When Drawing, These Keystrokes Are Available

- Hold down **Cmd** (Mac) or **Ctrl** (Windows) to get the **Direct Selection** tool .

- **Option–click** (Mac) or **Alt–click** (Windows) on an anchor point to change from a curve to a corner point.

- **Option–drag** (Mac) or **Alt–drag** (Windows) from an anchor point (while drawing a path) to switch from a straight line to a curve, or to simply change direction.

- To finish a path at a corner, hold down **Option** (Mac) or **Alt** (Windows) and drag from the last anchor point.

Blending Modes

Keep these terms in mind as you read the following descriptions of blend modes:

Base Color: The original color in the image.

Blend Color: The color being applied with the painting or editing tool.

Result Color: The color resulting from the blend.

Normal & Painting Blending Modes

- The **Normal** blending mode edits or paints each pixel to make it the result color. This is the default mode. (Normal mode is called Threshold when you're working with a bitmapped or indexed-color image.)

- The **Dissolve** blending mode edits or paints each pixel to make it the result color. However, the result color is a random replacement of the pixels with the base color or the blend color, depending on the opacity at any pixel location.

- The **Behind** blending mode edits or paints only on the transparent part of a layer. This mode works only in layers with Lock Transparency deselected and is analogous to painting on the back of transparent areas on a sheet of acetate.

- The **Clear** blending mode edits or paints each pixel and makes it transparent. This mode is available for the Line tool (when fill region is selected), the Paint Bucket tool, the Brush tool, the Pencil tool, the Fill command, and the Stroke command. You must be in a layer with Lock Transparency deselected to use this mode.

Darkening Blending Modes

- The **Darken** blending mode looks at the color information in each channel and selects the base or blend color—whichever is darker—as the result color. Pixels lighter than the blend color are replaced, and pixels darker than the blend color do not change.

- The **Multiply** blending mode looks at the color information in each channel and multiplies the base color by the blend color. The result color is always a darker color. Multiplying any color with black produces black. Multiplying any color with white leaves the color unchanged. When you're painting with a color other than black or white, successive strokes with a painting tool produce progressively darker colors. The effect is similar to drawing on the image with multiple magic markers.

- The **Color Burn** blending mode looks at the color information in each channel and darkens the base color to reflect the blend color by increasing the contrast. Blending with white produces no change.

- The **Linear Burn** blending mode looks at the color information in each channel and darkens the base color to reflect the blend color by decreasing the brightness. Blending with white produces no change.

Blending Modes

- The **Darker Color** blending mode compares the total of all channel values for the blend and base color and displays the lower value color. Darker Color does not produce a third color, which can result from the Darken blend, because it chooses the lowest channel values from both the base and the blend color to create the result color.

Lightening Blending Modes

- The **Lighten** blending mode looks at the color information in each channel and selects the base or blend color—whichever is lighter—as the result color. Pixels darker than the blend color are replaced, and pixels lighter than the blend color do not change.

- The **Screen** blending mode looks at each channel's color information and multiplies the inverse of the blend and base colors. The result color is always a lighter color. Screening with black leaves the color unchanged. Screening with white produces white. The effect is similar to projecting multiple photographic slides on top of each other.

- The **Color Dodge** blending mode looks at the color information in each channel and brightens the base color to reflect the blend color by decreasing the contrast. Blending with black produces no change.

- The **Linear Dodge (Add)** blending mode looks at the color information in each channel and brightens the base color to reflect the blend color by increasing the brightness. Blending with black produces no change.

- The **Lighter Color** blending mode compares the total of all channel values for the blend and base color and displays the higher value color. Lighter Color does not produce a third color, which can result from the Lighten blend, because it chooses the highest channel values from both the base and blend color to create the result color.

Contrast Blending Modes

- The **Overlay** blending mode multiplies or screens the colors, depending on the base color. Patterns or colors overlay the existing pixels while preserving the highlights and shadows of the base color. The base color is not replaced but is mixed with the blend color to reflect the lightness or darkness of the original color.

- The **Soft Light** blending mode darkens or lightens the colors, depending on the blend color. The effect is similar to shining a diffused spotlight on the image. If the blend color (light source) is lighter than 50% gray, the image is lightened as if it were dodged. If the blend color is darker than 50% gray, the image is darkened as if it were burned in. Painting with pure black or white produces a distinctly darker or lighter area but does not result in pure black or white.

Blending Modes

- The **Hard Light** blending mode multiplies or screens the colors, depending on the blend color. The effect is similar to shining a harsh spotlight on the image. If the blend color (light source) is lighter than 50% gray, the image is lightened, as if it were screened. This is useful for adding highlights to an image. If the blend color is darker than 50% gray, the image is darkened, as if it were multiplied. This is useful for adding shadows to an image. Painting with pure black or white results in pure black or white.

- The **Vivid Light** blending mode burns or dodges the colors by increasing or decreasing the contrast, depending on the blend color. If the blend color (light source) is lighter than 50% gray, the image is lightened by decreasing the contrast. If the blend color is darker than 50% gray, the image is darkened by increasing the contrast.

- The **Linear Light** blending mode burns or dodges the colors by decreasing or increasing the brightness, depending on the blend color. If the blend color (light source) is lighter than 50% gray, the image is lightened by increasing the brightness. If the blend color is darker than 50% gray, the image is darkened by decreasing the brightness.

- The **Pin Light** blending mode replaces the colors, depending on the blend color. If the blend color (light source) is lighter than 50% gray, pixels darker than the blend color are replaced, and pixels lighter than the blend color do not change. If the blend color is darker than 50% gray, pixels lighter than the blend color are replaced, and pixels darker than the blend color do not change. This is useful for adding special effects to an image.

- The **Hard Mix** blending mode adds the red, green, and blue channel values of the blend color to the RGB values of the base color. If the resulting sum for a channel is 255 or greater, it receives a value of 255; if less than 255, a value of 0. Therefore, all blended pixels have red, green, and blue channel values of either 0 or 255. This changes all pixels to primary colors: red, green, blue, cyan, yellow, magenta, white, or black.

Inversion or Comparison Blending Modes

- The **Difference** blending mode looks at the color information in each channel and subtracts either the blend color from the base color or the base color from the blend color, depending on which has the greater brightness value. Blending with white inverts the base color values; blending with black produces no change.

- The **Exclusion** blending mode creates an effect similar to but lower in contrast than the Difference mode. Blending with white inverts the base color values. Blending with black produces no change.

Blending Modes

- The **Subtract** blending mode looks at the color information in each channel and subtracts the blend color from the base color. In 8- and 16-bit images, any resulting negative values are clipped to zero.

- The **Divide** blending mode looks at the color information in each channel and divides the blend color from the base color.

Color Blending Modes

- The **Hue** blending mode creates a result color with the luminance and saturation of the base color and the hue of the blend color.

- The **Saturation** blending mode creates a result color with the luminance and hue of the base color and the saturation of the blend color. Painting with this mode in an area with no saturation (black, white, or gray) causes no change.

- The **Color** blending mode creates a result color with the luminance of the base color and the hue and saturation of the blend color. This preserves the gray levels in the image and is useful for coloring monochrome images and for tinting color images.

- The **Luminosity** blending mode creates a result color with the hue and saturation of the base color and the luminance of the blend color. This mode creates an inverse effect from that of the Color mode.